GREAT COMPOSERS

BEETHOVEN

GREAT COMPOSERS

BEETHOVEN

ROBIN MAY

HAMLYN

First published in 1990 by
The Hamlyn Publishing Group Limited
a division of the Octopus Publishing Group
Michelin House, 81 Fulham Road, London SW3 6RB
and distributed for them by
Octopus Distribution Services Limited
Rushden, Northamptonshire NN10 9RZ

ISBN 0 600 56446 0

Produced by Mandarin Offset

Printed in Hong Kong

CONTENTS

THE
FIRST
TWENTY YEARS

Born into a musical family, with an early childhood later clouded by conflicting legends, Beethoven showed signs of genius by the end of his tenth year.

L udwig van Beethoven was probably born on 17 December 1770; he was definitely baptized on the following day, in Bonn, in what is now West Germany. ~~He spent many years of his life thinking that he had been born in 1772, because his harsh, often drunken father falsified his birth-date to give the impression that young Ludwig~~

A view of Bonn in Beethoven's lifetime.

Opposite
Beethoven's house in Bonn is now a museum as well as a shrine dedicated to his memory. He was born into a musician's family, in a town with a long musical tradition.

was an infant prodigy like Mozart. His mother was very different to his father. She was an affectionate woman, but bereft of smiles or laughter. She seems to have had little to laugh at.

'Seems' is the operative word, for Beethoven's early life remains obscured by contradictory legends, especially where his father is concerned. Was his father a lovable fellow and successful music teacher, or was he something of a monster who, in order to exploit the boy's obvious talents, and to create a marketable proposition, hauled him out of bed to make him practise night and day? Probably, he was a blend of both.

Beethoven was the second of seven children. The family was of Flemish descent. Their 'van' is not to be confused with the aristocratic 'von'. In her biography of the composer, Marion Scott has suggested that the family had Spanish blood, which certainly seems a possibility in view of some of the portraits of Beethoven. The Spanish had occupied the Netherlands for many years, especially the Catholic districts where the family had lived. Marion Scott cited Ernest Closson's *The Fleming in Beethoven* to support her opinion and also noted his considerable pride and quick temper.

Beethoven's grandfather was a much respected man with a fine bass voice. He left the town of Mechelen, where he had been a successful businessman as well as a singer, and, after other posts, reached Bonn, where he became a bass in the electoral chapel. He was in the choir of the Archbishop Elector of Cologne, who resided in Bonn, and he rose to be Kapellmeister. Electors tended to be younger sons of royal or semi-royal stock, approved of by the Pope, the Holy Roman Emperor and other church authorities. The ecclesiastical principalities were more tolerantly ruled than the secular ones. Fortunately, music was a binding factor whoever was in charge.

Beethoven's father Johann was born

Beethoven's father was a good musician who hoped that his son would become a prodigy.

around 1740 and was a good musician, whatever his character may have been. Young Ludwig was the second son, the first having survived only five days. There would be five more children, but only two reached manhood, Caspar and Nikolaus. Beethoven left school aged eleven, which explains his lack of prowess in spelling, writing and multiplication, also basic arithmetic. He never did learn to multiply. Worse, as far as the family was concerned, was his failure to become a prodigy. It seems that his father was a severe teacher, certainly a demanding one. Whether his demands were so unreasonable as to make him a fiend, a bully who locked Ludwig in the cellar, we are unlikely now to know.

A NEW TEACHER

The year 1779 was important for Beethoven, for his father ceased to be his only teacher. Tobias Pfeifer, a fine musician, gave him music lessons while lodging at the Beethoven house and a relation taught him the violin and viola, but the key event of that year for Beethoven was finding himself in the hands of an excellent teacher, Christian Neefe, the musical director of the Elector's theatrical troupe. By 1781 Neefe was the court organist, and the

Above *The death of Beethoven's mother was a cruel blow for Ludwig to bear.*

Left *Christian Gottlob Neefe was an admirable teacher for the young Beethoven, whose assistant he became and for whom he sometimes deputized when still under 12 years of age*

9

next year Beethoven became Neefe's assistant and acted as his deputy when Neefe was away on business. He was 11 years old.

Happily, Neefe not only taught him but wrote about him in the influential music journal, *Magazin der Musik*. In the issue which appeared on 2 March 1783, Neefe extolled the skill and power of Beethoven's piano-playing and sight-reading and reported that Beethoven was being trained in composition. He revealed that the boy had written nine variations on a march by Ernst Dressler and remarked on his youthful genius. He hoped that Beethoven would travel. If he continued as he had begun he would be a second Mozart.

That constant phenomenon, the fickle finger of fate, was to deal Beethoven some savage blows, but on this occasion it did him proud. People noticed him. He began to deputize for the Kapellmeister when he was away, becoming temporarily the orchestra's harpsichordist. This enabled him to get to know the operatic repertoire. All in all, 1783 became a modest but significant *annus mirabilis* for the youth, for he also had three sonatas published, all for the piano.

While he was working for Neefe, he was not paid a salary, despite his becoming assistant to the court organist. The Elector's death could have put paid to his hopes of advancement altogether, for the new Elector was a powerful man, being the brother of the Emperor Joseph II, and economy was his watchword. Neefe's salary was cut. However Beethoven benefitted, because he was given a proper salary. He was not overworked and found he had time to compose.

Bonn remained a backwater even with the Emperor's brother in charge. Beethoven experienced personal tragedy when his much-loved mother died, and his father's career began going downhill, partly because his voice was deteriorating. But Beethoven's own star was rising.

Neefe's belief that Beethoven should travel came to pass in 1787, before his mother died. His destination was to be Vienna. Authority must have approved and he left Bonn. It seems certain that he met and played to Mozart, and tradition has it that he had some lessons from him. Mozart may have prophesied that the youth would make a great name for himself. However,

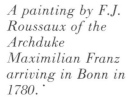

A painting by F.J. Roussaux of the Archduke Maximilian Franz arriving in Bonn in 1780.

Delacroix's famous painting Liberty leading the people. *The French Revolution inspired the world of the arts all over Europe, at least in its early days.*

Beethoven had to hurry back to Bonn when news reached him that his mother was ill. He found her dying of tuberculosis. It was a shattering blow for the lonely youth, who remembered her with love, recalling her as his best friend. Meanwhile, his character revealed itself publicly, for he declared himself head of the family and asked for and obtained half his father's salary in order to look after his brothers.

A happier period began, perhaps the happiest of his life so far. He was now a viola player in both the opera and the chapel orchestras, and made and kept some good friends among the musicians, especially Franz Ries, who became both his pupil and biographer.

EARLY COMMISSIONS

When news of the death of the enlightened Emperor Joseph II reached Bonn, Beethoven was asked to compose a suitable cantata. Though this was not performed, another was written for the accession of Leopold II. Again it was not played. However, in 1791 the influential Count Waldstein commissioned him to compose a ballet. It was the first – and a most important in view of their later friendship – of many contacts Beethoven would have with the aristocracy. The first truly independent composer was to benefit significantly from his upper-class introductions, and many of these enlightened enthusiasts admired him for his genius and, in many cases, became his friends. They liked him and sympathized with him, especially in the dark days that were to come.

Beethoven's powers as a pianist and improviser became even better known. The shy young man never lacked for friends. He found a second home with the van Breuning family, the widowed Frau seeing to it that he not only taught her children but their

wealthy friends. Young Count Waldstein gave him a fine piano.

In 1790, the great Haydn passed through Bonn on his way to London. The Elector made him welcome. It is not known if Beethoven met him. However, when Haydn was returning from London in 1792, the Bonn players gave him a breakfast at Godesburg, a local beauty spot, and there the young composer – so it is said – showed Haydn a cantata that impressed him very much. Some say that this occurred on Haydn's first visit. Whatever the truth, it

was now that, with the Elector's permission and financial aid, Beethoven set out for Vienna, crossing Europe as the French Revolution was approaching its height. He was to reach Vienna two months before Louis XVI was guillotined in Paris. Beethoven, now a young man of 22, for the second time reached the musical capital of Europe, not to visit, as before, but to stay. His friends had written in an album their feelings for him, Count Waldstein prophesying that he would receive Mozart's spirit from Haydn's hands.

Left *The old Burgtheater in Vienna. In 1800, Beethoven gave his first public benefit concert in this theatre.*

Above *The Archduke Maximilian Franz, Elector of Cologne, who lived in Bonn, was an important patron of Beethoven.*

THE
FIRST
VIENNA PERIOD

No city could better have nurtured the talent of Beethoven than Vienna, where his genius as a pianist and composer was recognised by a music-loving arisistocracy.

The Vienna that Beethoven reached in 1792 was an exeptionally musical city; indeed it is hard to believe that any city, even the Vienna of our century, has been so dominated and overwhelmed by the power and glory of music.

It was an age *in excelsis* of the piano virtuoso, and of an aristocracy who not only loved music and admired fervently the great performers of the day, but also played alongside them in their palaces and homes.

Beethoven made an immediate impact on this world. Not only was he a total master of the piano, but in an age when improvisation was widely admired and an art form in itself, he was soon recognized as the supreme expert of this art. In the enchanted world that he found himself inhabiting, Beethoven's humble beginnings were ignored.

Yet Beethoven was not satisfied with mere acceptance. He demanded equality with the aristocracy, not the equality of the licensed Fool at court, but the real thing. He won it, and it was not only a succession of well-born ladies who responded to his mag-

Opposite *An ivory miniature of Beethoven made in 1803.*

Left *The great Joseph Haydn may have met the young Beethoven in 1790. He definitely met him when Haydn stopped in Bonn on his way back from London in 1792. Bonn's musicians gave Haydn an open-air breakfast.*

15

Right *J.B. Cramer,*
a pianist whom
even the
demanding
Beethoven
admired.

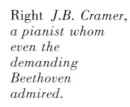

Below *Muzio*
Clementi, a
notable composer
and pianist, who
was also a music
publisher. He and
Beethoven knew
each other and
Clementi's London
edition of the
Emperor *concerto*
was the first to be
published.

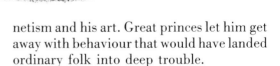

netism and his art. Great princes let him get away with behaviour that would have landed ordinary folk into deep trouble.

His timing was perfect. The *zeitgeist* – the current climate of opinion – favoured him. The two virtuosi, Clementi and Cramer, were entertaining the nobility at this particular moment. Mozart had died in 1791 and Beethoven was ready to take his place. As well as music in the aristocrat's salons, there were even a few public concerts, though fewer than London or Paris enjoyed.

In an age when improvisation was an art form which inspired players and the public alike, Beethoven was one of the most thrilling and inspirational practitioners. Carl Czerny, no mean composer as well as being Beethoven's pupil, the teacher of Liszt and a still-renowned writer of piano studies, called Beethoven's improvisations dazzling and amazing. They had a dramatic effect upon his audiences. The old theatrical cliche about there not being a dry eye in the house was frequently true of his playing. Indeed, his performances were supported almost like some of today's pop concerts.

Czerny not only tells us of the beauty and originality of his music inspirations, but also relates that at the end of an improvisation he was liable to laugh noisily and to tease his listeners about their reactions. He would actually call out to them: 'You're a crowd of idiots!' On occasion he seemed annoyed and called his public a bunch of spoiled children.

Clearly, in a later age, he might have starred in music hall, vaudeville or cabaret, had he wished.

Yet Beethoven's attitude to his art was serious and was born of his intellect and his heart. Czerny noted how assured and pertinent his musical utterances were.

The heart of musical Vienna was the salon, and there Beethoven established himself as king; not at first of course, but his reputation spread fast. His relationship with Haydn was uneasy, personally as well as

Carl Czerny, Beethoven's pupil and the teacher of Liszt, greatly admired Beethoven's prowess as an improviser.

Right *A portrait of the Princess Esterházy, wife of one of Beethoven's patrons. The latter had a low opinion of a Mass that Beethoven had written for him.*

Below *The home of Prince Esterházy at Eisenstadt.*

professionally it would seem, though it continued until 1794. Haydn took him to Eisenstadt, where the composer's patron Prince Esterházy had his country home. Esterházy appears to have been kinder to the youthful Beethoven than some have claimed.

It seems that Haydn was slowing down and – understandably – was puzzled by his pupil's musical thoughts. Beethoven wanted tougher teaching than he got from the older composer and felt he was not understood. Even before Haydn's departure for England in 1794, Beethoven was looking for and finding other teachers, like Albrechtsberger and the famous Salieri. Ferdinand Ries, son of his friend in the Bonn orchestra, stated that all his teachers valued him highly but criticized his methods of studying and his self-sufficient ways.

FIRST PUBLIC CONCERTS

When Haydn left for London in 1794, the impatient, aspiring young Beethoven was in a position to help himself. His first public appearance was in 1795 in Vienna. The concert was a public one in aid of the widows of musicians, and the programme included the young composer's B flat piano concerto, known to us as his Second Piano Concerto. It was actually written first, and is clearly less mature than those which followed it. Yet the last movement is unmistakably Beethoven, a charmingly high-spirited finale with portents of delights to come. The date was 29 March. On the following day, he improvised publicly, and on the last day of the month he played a Mozart piano concerto at a musical event organized by the composer's widow.

Beethoven's growing fame had a remarkable effect on his lifestyle. His noble patrons, most notably Prince Karl Lichnowsky, who had had lessons from Mozart, became part of the pattern of his life. The prince and his wife were ardent champions and true friends. They put up with his sometimes wildly offensive behaviour and they certainly deserved the immortality that his dedications have given them. They were used to aspiring artists, many of whom stayed with them from time to time, and forgave Beethoven his notable unpunctuality, realizing that creative people often keep erratic hours. The prince and his friends coped with the blazing genius in their midst with rare understanding.

In 1796, Beethoven visited Prague and

Constanze Mozart, the composer's widow, who in 1795 organized a concert at which Beethoven played.

Berlin, impressing the musical King Frederick William of Prussia, a musician himself. Beethoven wrote two cello sonatas for Duport, a cellist in the royal orchestra, and the King tried to get him to stay in Berlin. Beethoven's refusal was an interesting one. He was not prepared to live among spoilt children, who wept emotionally instead of clapping. Goethe fell foul of him for similar reasons. The great poet and dramatist appears to have been struck dumb.

Beethoven's reactions to his audiences varied. To break an awestruck silence he had induced, he would sometimes, as noted, burst out laughing. However, once, when a sprig of the aristocracy came into a room where Beethoven's pupil Ferdinand Ries was playing, Beethoven grabbed his hands, slammed the piano shut, and dragged Ries away, saying loudly: 'You must not play before pigs.'

Nor were his players left unscathed if they were below his standards. Faced with a scratch or ill-disciplined orchestra, Beethoven was likely to explode, even after just a single rehearsal. If they did not yet have the ability to give him what he wanted, they had to bear the brunt of his wrath.

His wrath was very much part of his character. One of his friends was Georg August Griesinger, a diplomat and a biographer of Haydn. When they were both young, with Beethoven only known as a pianist and his friend an attaché, they met on one occasion at the house of Prince Lobkowitz. A self-important art connoisseur started talking to Beethoven about the social station and attitudes of poets. Beethoven decided

An early Beethoven concert notice.

Left *King Frederick William II of Prussia, a gifted amateur musician, who was impressed by Beethoven's gifts as a pianist.*

Below *A view of Berlin, c. 1814.*

that some frank speaking was in order. He announced his dislike of arguing with publishers and said how much better it would be if he could discover one who would pay him an annual salary, the publisher having the right to publish all his works. He believed that both Goethe and Handel enjoyed or had enjoyed such arrangements. The connoisseur decided it was high time that the young man be shown his place. 'You are neither a Goethe nor a Handel,' he pronounced, 'and there is not the slightest reason to think that you ever will be. Such intellects are not born into the world a second time.'

Beethoven gritted his teeth, launched a scornful glare at his tormentor and did not speak another word to him. The Prince tried to calm the young composer down, saying to Beethoven that he did not believe any insult had been intended. 'It is traditional for most older folk to believe that younger men could never achieve as much as the old or the dead.'

'Alas, that's true,' replied Beethoven, 'but I refuse to have any truck with those who won't believe in me because I have not yet achieved a wide reputation.'

Franz Wegeler, who became a doctor and, later, a biographer of Beethoven's early life, recalled how he was never out of love; indeed, he stated that his friend made conquests that even an Adonis would have found difficult or impossible. In a short book there is no room for a list of his probable conquests. The 'Moonlight' Sonata he dedicated to Countess Giulietta

Beethoven's pupil, Countess Giulietta Guicciardi, whom he loved. After he died this picture was found among his belongings.

Therese, Countess von Brunswick, painted by J.B. Lampi.

Guicciardi, and he proposed to her cousin Josephine. Therese and Josephine von Brunswick were two more of many who meant much to him. Pictures of the young composer help explain some of his success. He had a handsome, powerful face. W.J. Mahler's portrait of the composer at 44 shows also a melancholy in the sensitive features.

DEAFNESS

In the last two years of the 18th century Beethoven discovered that he was going deaf. By 1801 there could be no doubt of it and it was getting worse. It has been suggested that typhus was the cause. A buzzing in his ears seems to have been the first symptom. The trouble was not at first constant, though the buzzing sometimes drove him into a frenzy. His living as a pianist was in jeopardy, slow as the process of losing his hearing was. On bad days his musical judgement was hopelessly flawed, for inevitably fortissimo and pianissimo became blurred. His conducting was equally affected, resulting ultimately in the need to have an additional conductor to stand behind him and provide an accurate beat.

He opened his heart to his good friend Wegeler about his deafness in a most moving letter written in the summer of 1801. Everything except the one all-important matter of his hearing was going well. Some doctors claimed that his abdomen was the cause of his complaint, while one 'medical idiot' told him that he needed cold baths. Meanwhile, he was being weakened by dysentery. Lukewarm Danube water was recommended for bathing in, which he believed was helping him, also pills for the stomach. Almond oil was being poured into his ears, but his hearing got worse. A kind of tea was tried, but caused a whistling and roaring in his ears. Meanwhile, he brooded as to what his enemies would say about a deaf composer.

Already, he was having to strain to hear the actors in the theatres, even when he positioned himself near the front. Yet he could not endure being yelled at. At this grim moment he fell in love and seems to have been truly happy for a while, writing to Wegeler of some 'moments of total bliss'.

At other times he brooded about the business of being a composer. In a letter to another friend, Franz Anton Hoffmeister, he propounded that there should be just one art market in the world, an art exchange where the artist would be given what he needed. He objected that he had to be a businessman as well as an artist.

Fortunately, he had never lacked courage. Back in 1795, before there was any hint of deafness, he wrote in a diary that even with the frailties of his body, his spirit would be indomitable. It nearly always was.

Beethoven's predicament was posterity's gain. Forced to abandon his public career, he was thrown back on his inner resources, despite times of suicidal despair. He concentrated on composing. His depression and downright misery could not break his spirit,

as the Heiligenstadt Testament shows. This resulted in his glorious second period from about 1800 to 1812, when he produced so many of his greatest works.

From now onwards it would be hard for him to be completely at ease among his fellow musicians and the sympathetic admirers of his own class who enjoyed his jokes. He took umbrage easily but was usually ready to apologize and admit that he was to blame.

THE SECOND PERIOD

In 1802, he faced the possibility that he would lose his hearing altogether. He drew up the document named for the village of Heiligenstadt on the outskirts of Vienna where he sometimes stayed in the summer. It was addressed to his brothers and was a brave statement, albeit couched in melodramatic terms. He was resolved to accept his destiny, whatever it was. He was filled with the desire to do good. Utterly humiliated, feeling totally misunderstood, he was resigned and yet was resolved to create even more powerful music. He could not leave the world before producing the music he felt bound to compose. So he began his second period, the period in which the

Beethoven's hearing aids – evidence of his tragic affliction.

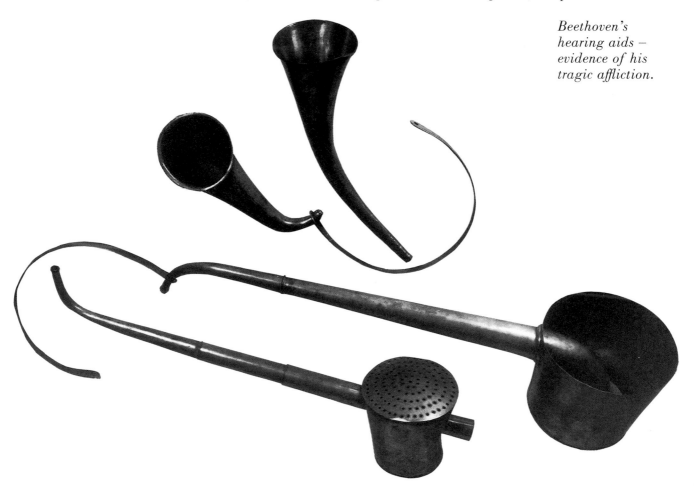

*In this house in
Heiligenstadt, now
part of Vienna,
Beethoven wrote
his Testament in
1802. It showed
that he had come
to terms with the
tragedy of his
deafness and
everything that it
implied.*

*A page of the
Heiligenstadt
document, which
was found after
his death.*

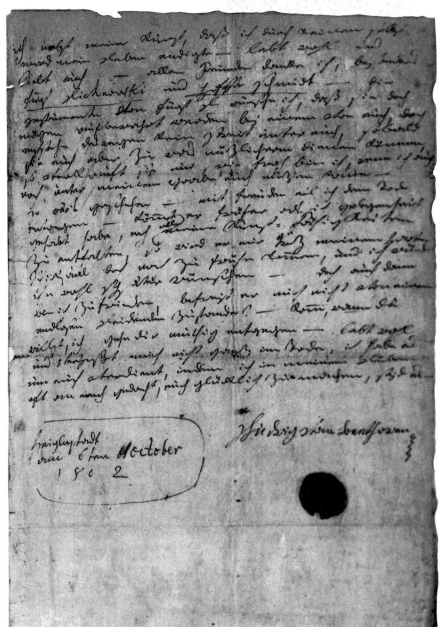

man of destiny was to gloriously fulfil himself.

Only those with little imagination can fail to respond to words he wrote to his friend Wegeler, which can hardly be written off as melodramatic under such circumstances. 'I will seize fate by the throat' is one promise, while in the other he states that if only he could rid himself of his affliction he would embrace the whole world.

The changes in Beethoven's music at this unhappy but defiant period are so striking that even comparative newcomers to music soon begin to grasp them. He did not strive for the 'music of the future' as Wagner would do. He was no romantic revolutionary, but he was a trailblazer and his music became heroic in character.

He did not become totally deaf until 1819, but he had endured years of anguish by then, symbolized by wrecked instruments as he strove to hear his playing.

The years of 1803 and 1804 were each an *annus mirabilis*. One April day in 1803 his Second Symphony and Third Piano Concerto were given their first performances at a public concert, and during these years two of his greatest sonatas, the *Waldstein* and the *Appassionata*, were composed.

The long struggle to get his only opera

Prince Razumovsky, a notable patron of Beethoven who dedicated several of his greatest works to him.

Thomas Lawrence's portrait of the Duke of Wellington. Beethoven's Wellington's Victory, which commemorates the defeat of Napoleon's forces at the Battle of Vitoria, is a potboiler but enjoyable, nonetheless.

Fidelio right, described later, lasted from 1805 to 1814.

The astounding period under discussion included the composition of his symphonies numbered 2 to 8, fourteen sonatas for the piano, the Razumovsky string quartets – the count of that name was Russian Ambassador in Vienna, a good musician and a discerning patron – and the very powerful overture to *Coriolan* (not the Shakespeare play but one by Heinrich Collin).

Beethoven did not write potboilers as a rule, but accepted a commission to write a piece to celebrate the victory of the Duke of Wellington over the French at Vitoria. This *Battle Symphony*, originally composed for a mechanical marvel called the Panharmonicum, the brain child of J.N. Maelzel, was

This porcelain ewer, depicting Wellington's victory at Vitoria, is now in his London home.

later turned into an orchestral piece. Naturally, it was a great success and it deserved to be, naive as it is. Beethoven knew what he was doing and was quite prepared to admit that it was the worst sort of programme music. But it is highly enjoyable. Cannons are a feature of this simple bit of 'realism', along with national anthems and musketry.

Landmarks abound in this extraordinary outpouring of genius that was Beethoven's second period, as the final chapter will show in some detail, but in this more general survey two particular landmarks must be noted. The first is the opening of the *Eroica* Symphony, surely the most gigantic step forward in the history of music, including Beethoven's own. The breathtaking advance musically in the very first bars was a

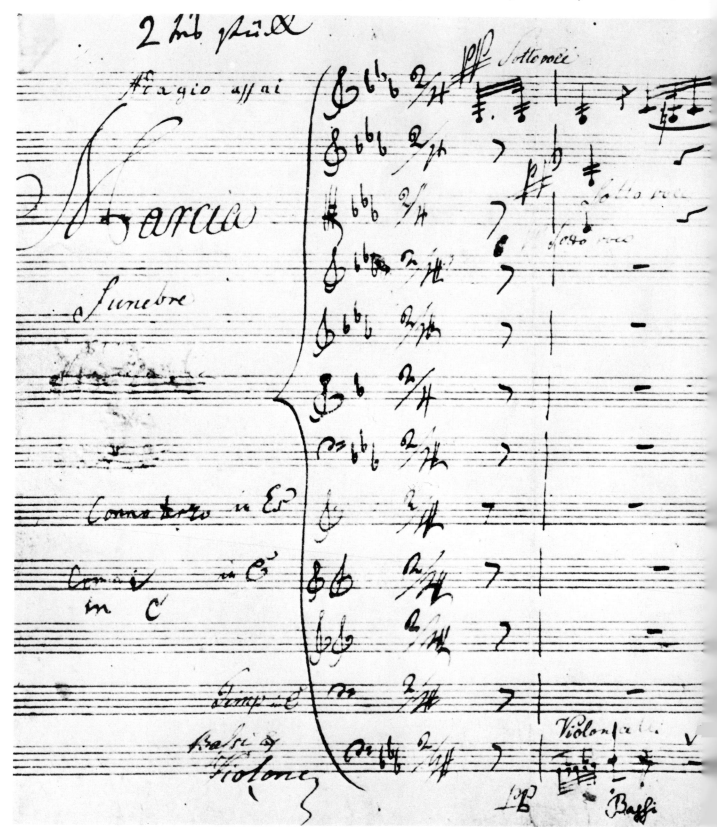

thrilling and dramatic start to a new era. Forgetting all Napoleonic associations, purely as music the revolution is profound. The tremendous second movement, and heroic and deeply stirring funeral march, is almost as revolutionary.

Another revolution came with the Fifth Symphony, which raised the last movement, which had so often before been lightweight compared to the first, to the status of genuine climax of the work. The apotheosis of the revolution was reached in the choral finale of the Ninth Symphony. The French composer and teacher Lesueur erupted to Berlioz, who himself was almost as revolutionary a composer as Beethoven: 'Let me get out! I need air! It is incredible! Marvellous!'

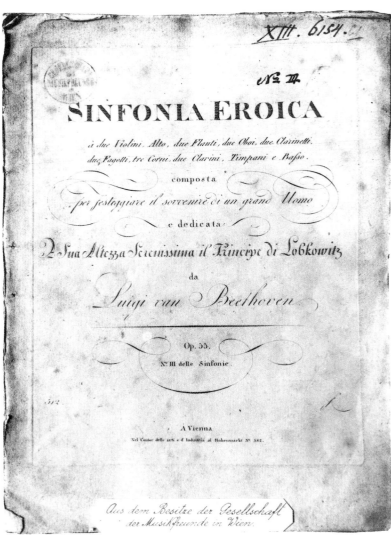

Left *The manuscript of the opening bars of the* Eroica *symphony's magnificent slow movement.*

Above *The title page of the first edition of the* Eroica *symphony, Beethoven's Third.*

Beethoven profoundly admired Goethe, Germany's supreme poet and philosopher. His incidental music to the poet's *Egmont* dates from 1810. Beethoven had been invited to meet Goethe, but the meeting did not occur until 1812.

THE SOCIAL MAN

An excellent word portrait of Beethoven has come down to us from a Frau von Bernhard, who came to Vienna to complete her piano studies. She met him at the home of Prince Lichnowsky and he made a vivid impression on her.

Whenever he arrived, he would poke his head around the door to check if anyone whom he disliked was there. He struck her as plain and small with a pock-marked face that was both red and ugly. His darkish hair hung somewhat shaggily around his face. His clothes were very ordinary in the fashion of the day and he spoke in a rather common way in a strong dialect. The good lady was clearly rather a snob and found Beethoven vulgar and uncultivated. By Viennese standards he was but, happily, most of the nobility were anything but haughty in his presence. Frau von Bernhard noted that the mother of Princess Lichnowsky, Countess Thun, went down on her knees to beseech him to play something. Alas, on this occasion he stayed slumped on the sofa.

The frau had other memories – of Haydn and Salieri sitting on the sofa in the height of fashion, while Beethoven would come in looking like someone from the other side of the Rhine, in other words, ill-dressed.

To the eternal credit of the Austrian aristocracy, most of them seemed honoured to have such a giant in their midst. Accord-

A portrait of Goethe, the great German dramatist, writer and natural philosopher, whom Beethoven first met in 1812.

David's famous portrait of the young Napoleon Bonaparte, who appointed him court painter in 1804.

Count Moritz Lichnovsky, who treated Beethoven like a true friend and saw to it that others treated him well.

ing to Czerny, Prince Lichnowsky treated Beethoven like a friend and a brother and saw to it that virtually the whole of the Austrian aristocracy did the same.

Always likely to see through the wrong sort of flattery, Beethoven was none too pleased when the pianist Madame Cibbini gushed that he was surely the only composer who had never written anything feeble or unworthy of notice. Beethoven let the pianist off quite lightly, merely observing that there was a lot he would like to take out if he had the chance. Naturally, he complained when the public chose the wrong

music – in his opinion – to adore.

Czerny has left us with a number of such talking points. He even changed his mind for the second time about Napoleon. Having worshipped him originally, he famously denounced him, as most music-lovers know. What is less well known is the fact that he changed his mind yet again and went back to admiring him, perhaps because of the shortage of remarkable leaders in the 1820s.

His musical criticisms were often brilliant and subtle. Weber's grandiose *Euryanthe*, as those who have experienced it in the theatre will know, is not very stageworthy.

Beethoven's comment was that Weber had put far too much effort into the piece. He would have made a superb music critic. All he would have needed in his later days, of course, would have been the score, enough even though the joy of sound had been banished from him.

He never hesitated to stick up for his rights. His letter to the Archduke Rudolph when *Fidelio* had been staged without a thought about payment to its composer was witty, restrained and diplomatic. Two centuries on he still gives the impression of being a splendidly surprising man.

Above *Carl Weber, whose opera* Der Freischütz *(1821) was much admired by Beethoven.*

Left *The Razumovsky palace in Vienna, where Prince Razumovsky was the Russian Ambassador.*

33

CELEBRITY

In the first 20 years of the 19th century, when his genius was in full flower, Beethoven's belief in himself sustained him in face of increasing deafness.

I n 1809, Vienna had fallen to the French. Beethoven had covered his head with pillows during the bombardment. His ears had to be protected. Once, like so many Europeans, he had believed in Bonaparte. He had seemed a symbol of hope and freedom, indeed the *Eroica* was originally dedicated to the great Corsican. But when Bonaparte proclaimed himself the Emperor Napoleon, the composer's reaction was fierce. In anguish, he seized the title page, ripped out the fallen idol's name and stated on the score that it was composed to celebrate the memory of a great man. The sight of a French officer had him clenching his fist and roaring that if he

Opposite A portrait of Beethoven in his early thirties by an unknown artist.

In 1809 Vienna fell to the French, to Beethoven's horror. His admiration for Napoleon vanished for ever.

Bettina von Brentano helped bring Goethe and Beethoven together. She proved a lively and delightful friend.

was a general and knew as much about strategy as he did about counterpoint, he'd give him and his like something to do!

Now at last came the famous meeting with Goethe, set up by a highly intelligent and attractive young woman of eighteen, Bettina Brentano, who had been sending news of the composer to Goethe. She came of a very literary family but some of the letters that she alleged having received from Beethoven are considered her own inventions. However, she has left us a famous description of the state of his room in 1810 – a piano and a chaos of objects, but otherwise bare.

The meeting of the two mighty minds took place at Teplitz at the time of Napoleon's crossing the border into Russia. Goethe viewed Beethoven as the most self-contained, lively and sincere artist that he had ever met and could understand that his attitude to the world was a singular one. Yet as he got to know him better, Goethe saw a different person. He was astonished by his talent but considered his personality absolutely uncontrolled. Goethe could understand Beethoven's views on a detestable world, but was sorry that that resulted in

The incident on the Promenade at Teplitz: Goethe bows to the Emperor and Empress; Beethoven does not.

Beethoven could rejoice that Napoleon's star was on the wain.

everyone else being affected by his attitude. Yet the poet felt he must be forgiven: his deafness was getting worse.

Beethoven is said to have behaved boorishly at Teplitz when the two artists met the Emperor and Empress on the Promenade, Goethe bowing politely while Beethoven charged forward, his arms folded. No doubt the story is embroidered, but he did complain to his publishers, Breitkopf and Härtel, that court air suited Goethe more than it should for a poet. Goethe never ceased to admire Beethoven, while Beethoven's idols remained Homer, Shakespeare, Plato – and Goethe.

THE DOMESTIC FRONT

The battle with life went on, successfully on the artistic front, but it must be noted that Beethoven's domestic arrangements were remarkable. It appears that in 35 years living in or on the outskirts of Vienna he managed to live in 33 different homes. He seems to have suffered from some form of wanderlust, for he was never poor in the way Mozart and Schubert were poor. He usually had several rooms, including one for his servants, to whom he behaved

Above *Countess Erdödy was a fine pianist and a valuable friend of Beethoven, before they fell out.*

Right *Lampi's portrait of Archbishop Rudolph, a good friend of the composer's as well as a pupil.*

both well and badly. The air must have rung with abuse and apologies, complete with handsome tips. Countess Erdödy stopped a servant leaving his over-demanding master by paying the man a secret wage to fortify himself against the strain. Beethoven is to be imagined in dressing-gown and nightshirt well into the afternoon working in his music room, the air filled with pipe-smoke, the room full of manuscripts. It has been suggested that he poured water over himself as a means of pulling himself together. If he did so, and ignored the occasional and inevitable waterfalls onto the apartment below, then the frequency with which he changed his lodgings becomes explicable.

Though the aristocracy were in general remarkably broad-minded about his behaviour, individuals must have been aghast from time to time. The courtiers who surrounded the Archduke Rudolph tried to get him to behave conventionally and he did promise to improve. But the strain was too great. At last he burst into the Archduke's presence and vehemently proclaimed that though he very much respected him, his courtiers were once again tutoring him. Rudolph was amused and ordered that the composer should behave as he wanted to.

His players suffered, too. On 22 December 1808 three major works were premiered at the Theater an der Wien – the C Minor and Pastoral Symphonies and the Choral Fantasy for piano, orchestra and chorus. During this last work the clarinetist mistakenly repeated eight bars, noted by everyone because the passage was an exposed one. Enraged, Beethoven abused the players so loudly and coarsely that all present heard him. 'From the beginning!' he then ordered and all went well, but afterwards he started berating them. Some swore that they would never play for him again, but when he produced a new work, their curiosity got the better of their rage and they returned to play for him once more. Waiters, too, had reason to fear him. He once flung a plate of roast beef and sauce at a waiter's head. Yet they finally came to tolerate his wildly veering behaviour and his absent-mindedness, and staffs tolerated him, even when he forgot to pay the bill.

He was prepared to talk about his methods of composition. A young composer, Louis Schlösser, asked him about them. Beethoven told him that he carried his ideas about for a long time before writing them down. He trusted his own memory and was convinced he would not forget them – his absent-mindedness, of course, was about mundane matters. He was prepared to change a great deal, cut and start again, until the result satisfied him. This was a 'working-out' period, all in his head, while the basic conception grew and grew. When he could see the whole, all that remained was getting it down on paper. There was no problem about having several works in the process of creation at once. His ideas came to him unbidden. He felt he could grasp them with his hands, sometimes walking in the woods, sometimes in the still of the night. Tones came to him as a sound, a surge and a roar. Then they stood before him as notes.

GUARDIANSHIP

Thanks to his famous sketch-books we can follow the process from the very birth of his ideas to the fulfilment of them. Yet for a crucial period his muse seems to have deserted him. The years 1805–12 had been gloriously creative, but between 1813 and 1819, he composed comparatively little. It cannot be blamed only on the difficulties with his nephew Karl, whom we have yet to meet; that was a cross he had to bear from 1815. The profound emotional disappointment of a failed love affair in 1815 provides part of the reason. Poor health and the approach of total deafness is enough to complete the picture, and to explain the creative loss. Clinical depression surely assailed him, well over a century before it could be treated. That he won his fight is proved beyond measure by the final incomparable years of creation. Yet these 'silent years' were not totally without music. His great *Hammerklavier* sonata dates from this period, also two cello sonatas, a few orchestral pieces and the much-maligned *Battle Symphony*.

Meanwhile there was his nephew Karl.

Before describing the crisis, it must be stressed that Beethoven was enjoying great popularity and making a considerable fortune, and was even being made presentable by the devoted ministrations of Frau Nanette Streicher and her piano-maker husband, along with other devoted persons. She saw to it that he had good and, equally important, faithful servants. Then disaster struck.

Beethoven's brother Karl died in 1815, leaving him as the guardian of his nephew, who was also called Karl. Beethoven had no time for Karl's mother, Johanna, whom he had long since written off as an immoral woman, but he regarded his brother's request as a sacred trust. From that moment he was more than an uncle to the youth and did his best to protect the boy from her influence. The result would be a disaster. Johanna had not been appointed guardian in the will made by Karl, but a codicil had been added on the day before Karl died making Johanna the child's co-guardian.

Beethoven now felt he had a son. He even underlined a line in his copy of *Othello*: 'I had rather to adopt a son than get it.' The boy was nine years old.

Beethoven did his best to be a good father to the boy, but the years ahead read like an emotional nightmare. He tried so hard, too hard, to do the right thing as he saw it, but the result makes sorry reading. There were law-suits to be fought over the child, a difficult and ungrateful youth, yet one sympathizes with the youngster also. He was almost suffocated by Beethoven's love for him, and there was no way that Karl could live up to his uncle's expectations. He was sent to a good school, but it was not a success and Beethoven unwisely decided to take charge of the boy's education. He told a friend that his house resembled a shipwreck. He loved the youth deeply, but suffered grievously because the love was not returned. He had to fight to keep the boy, who in 1819 was actually taken away from him, but after a long series of legal battles he got

Above *Nanette Streicher was the daughter of a noted piano-maker. She did her best to domesticate Beethoven – a struggle indeed.*

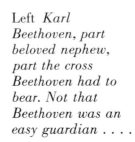

Left *Karl Beethoven, part beloved nephew, part the cross Beethoven had to bear. Not that Beethoven was an easy guardian . . . .*

him back. This was in 1820, by which time he was fulfilling his destiny as a composer once again.

IN CONCERT

An example of a Beethoven concert at this time must be given. The first performance of the Seventh Symphony took place on 29 November 1814 and was organized by his friends. The composer Louis Spohr left a vivid account of the event, which was devoted to new compositions. *Fidelio* had just had a successful revival. Now every musician in Vienna seemed bent on taking part in this new tribute to Beethoven.

Spohr noted Beethoven's way of conducting by means of a battery of 'peculiar movements with his body' (which would surely not surprise a modern audience).

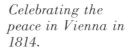

When he wanted a *piano* effect he would crouch lower and lower, while a *crescendo* saw him rising gradually. When the *forte* was due he leapt in the air, while a *piano* had him crouching. An extra strong *forte* had him shouting, a *sforzando* saw him hurling his arms out, having previously held them across his breast.

It was a great occasion, the reception for the Seventh Symphony signaling a tremendous success, so much so that the slow movement had to be played again. Despite Beethoven's inevitably uncertain conducting – it was quite clear to all that he could not hear the music – the performance went splendidly. When things did go wrong, the orchestral players were perfectly able to cope, as players are still wont to do today. So Beethoven's unexpected leap into the air under the impression that he had reached a *forte* only alarmed him and not his players. His good friends organized another concert

Celebrating the peace in Vienna in 1814.

Isabey's painting of the statesmen at the Congress of Vienna in 1814.

Louis (Ludwig) Spohr (1784–1859), a notable violinist, composer and conductor.

Franz Schubert, whose early death was a tragedy, so great was his achievement and promise.

with the same programme, and the receipts were a boon for the afflicted, indomitable composer.

During the years when his creative urge was low, he was not a recluse. He would drop into the publishing house of Steiner and Company for a pleasant hour or so in the morning twice a week. Other composers were there and a great deal of 'shop' was talked. Schubert, then a shy, obscure composer, and a musician friend of his, Hüttenbrenner, were sometimes there. Hüttenbrenner recalled later Beethoven's candid remarks, especially on Italian music; Schubert was too shy to approach him.

THE ECCENTRIC

B eethoven spent some months in the countryside outside Vienna every year. His love for the country was even more intense than the *Pastoral Symphony* may suggest to the listener. His deafness did not plague him, the stillness of the woods delighted him; indeed he regarded the country with religious fervour, as an entry in one of his notebooks shows. It was a consolation, a very real blessing, which enabled him to bear his endless burdens.

Meanwhile, when he was in Vienna he became one of the sights of the city, not least because he was usually lost in deep thought, or humming, or gesticulating. Children are sensitive to their parents' behaviour and appearance, so perhaps we can understand why young Karl was ashamed to be seen out with him, with his allegedly comic appearance. He was also a gift for street urchins to mock, as Dr Gerhard von Breuning recalled. The good doctor was, of course, proud to be seen in his company.

He was prepared to speak his mind about anything, politics included, at a time when it was dangerous to do so. One suspects that it would have required startling imprudence to land him in real trouble, but in a period of Austrian history when it was unwise to be radical in word or deed, he was quite prepared to criticize the authorities openly. For him, however, freedom was not simply a matter of politics.

Before we embark on Beethoven's final years – when his creative powers were more than restored – a light-hearted tale may be in order. In 1820 he was at Baden. Wandering about all day, he became lost – and hungry. He started looking into the windows of houses and the recipients of his stares called for the constable. Alas, the guardian of the

The Vienna woods, much loved by Beethoven and many other composers.

law did not believe he was Herr Beethoven and accused him of being a tramp. He was marched away and locked up.

Meanwhile, the local Commissioner of Police was enjoying a small party in the garden of a tavern. The constable arrived and told the Commissioner about his difficult prisoner who kept saying he was Beethoven, but was clearly a tramp, a ragamuffin, with no means of identification. 'Lock him up,' ordered the Commissioner, 'until the morning!'

At eleven o'clock that night, a policeman woke the Commissioner and told him that the prisoner insisted that the musical director of the Wiener Neustadt be summoned to identify him. The Commissioner got up and ordered that the tramp be brought to him. 'That *is* Beethoven,' he gasped, and took him to his own house. Beethoven was sent home next morning in the Commissioner's official coach.

Sketches of the composer by J.P. Lyser.

47

THE
FINAL DECADE

The 1820s found Beethoven famous at home and abroad. In these final years a relative fallow period ended with some of his mightiest works.

Though tormented by his deafness and his disastrous relationship with his nephew, Beethoven's fame and prestige were immense by the start of the 1820s. His renown by now was not confined to Austria and Germany. Since 1813, when it was founded, the Philharmonic Society of London – now the Royal Philharmonic Society – had been playing his music. Its members hoped that one day he would

Opposite *Franz Klein's fine bust of Beethoven dates from 1812.*

Left *London's Philharmonic Society's Orchestra in the Hanover Square concert hall. The orchestra did much to popularise Beethoven's music in England.*

compose for them, and later bought the rights of his Ninth Symphony, though, in the event, its premiere took place in Vienna.

The French also responded to his music, and Hector Berlioz, himself to write a critical study of the nine symphonies, noted that it was the public rather than the musicians who discovered the real content of his music. New Yorkers were responding to it by the 1820s. As for his fellow composers, Liszt, Weber and Rossini were among those who felt honoured to meet him, though Weber did not appreciate Beethoven's music at first and Beethoven had no time for Weber until, as will be noted, he discovered *Der Freischütz*. At first, too, Beethoven thought that Rossini was merely talented and melodious and that his music suited the frivolous and sensual age.

Beethoven's years of comparative silence were not idle ones. In 1817, he began work on the Ninth Symphony, though the genesis of its great choral finale is noted in his sketch books as early as 1798. As for the other huge masterwork, the *Missa Solemnis*, Beethoven began to compose it in 1818.

From time to time he still conducted, though the revival of *Fidelio* in 1822 proved that his conducting days were over. He still hoped to retain at least some of his hearing. Meanwhile, a new patron came into his life, the musical and very generous Russian Prince Golitsïn, who asked him for up to three quartets for the fee that he wished. It

Beethoven never lost his joy in nature. Mödling, south of Vienna, was one of his favourite spots.

50

was after a trip to Vienna that Golitsïn made his generous offer, which resulted in some of Beethoven's very finest music being created. His mind had already been on works in this form before the offer reached him.

In the event, there would be five great masterpieces, less well-known to the concert-going public than the works of his middle period, but esteemed by those who truly know them as among the very greatest achievements in the history of art. Prince Golitsïn was not alone in his admiration of the quartets. It is a mistaken legend that these masterpieces were beyond the ken of virtually all their first audiences. The Beethoven scholar, H.C. Robbins Landon, has

noted that documents show that 'this is one of those half-truths that seem to bedevil Beethoven biographers.'

One of Beethoven's closest friends was Ignaz Schuppanzigh, a brilliant violinist. He liked to direct performances in his capacity as first violinist. The story goes that Schuppanzigh told Beethoven at a rehearsal of one of the last quartets that a passage was virtually impossible to play. 'I can't be bothered about your wretched violin when I'm speaking to my God' was Beethoven's withering reply.

The composition of the quartets for Prince Golitsïn was an exciting period for Beethoven, whose imagination seems to have been in exceptional form. 'My dear fellow,' he would say to his violinist friend and drinking companion, Karl Holz, 'I've had another idea.' Holz's own idea was often for another drinking bout – this was for some months in the mid-1820s – which did Beethoven no good.

Beethoven's interest in younger composers was admirably genuine. He greatly admired the young Schubert, and it was no fault of his that the shy young man did not follow up his only attempt to visit him. He praised Rossini's *Barber of Seville* to the Italian composer in person.

Ignaz Schuppanzigh was a famous violinist and a great friend of Beethoven who was always at home with his fellow musicians.

AN
ENGLISH PORTRAIT

A portrait of Beethoven drawn by C.F.K. Klober in 1818.

O ne of the most vivid accounts of Beethoven was written by an English traveller, John Russell, in his *A Tour in Germany and Some of the Southern Provinces of the Austrian Empire in the Years 1820, 1821, 1822.* The book was published in 1825, while the composer was still alive. Noting that Beethoven was the most celebrated of the living composers, he wrote that he was lost to society because of his deafness, which had rendered him almost unsocial. Russell reported the 'neglect of his person'. He went on:

His features are strong and prominent; his eye is full of rude energy; his hair, which neither comb nor scissors seem to have visited for years, overshadows his broad brow in a quantity and confusion to which only the snakes round a Gorgon's head offer a parallel. His general behaviour does not ill accord with the unpromising exterior. Except when he is among his chosen friends, kindness or affability are not his characteristics. The total loss of hearing has deprived him of all the

pleasure which society can give and per- haps soured his temper. He used to frequent a particular cellar, where he spent the evenings in a corner, beyond the reach of all the chattering and disputation of a public room, drinking wine and beer, and eating cheese and red herrings, and studying the newspapers. One evening a person took a seat near him whose countenance did not please him. He looked hard at the stranger, and spat on the floor as if he had seen a toad . . . and spat again, his hair bristling gradually into more shaggy ferocity, till he closed the alternation of spitting and staring, by

fairly exclaiming, 'What a scoundrelly phiz!' and rushing out of the room. Even among his oldest friends he must be humoured like a wayward child . . . The moment he is seated at the piano, he is evidently unconscious that there is any- thing in existence but himself and his instrument . . . when playing very *piano* he often does not bring out a single note . . . .While his eye, and the almost imper- ceptible motion of his fingers show that he is following out the strain in his own soul through all its dying gradations, the instrument is actually as dumb as the musician is deaf.

A piano of Beethoven's. He ruined some, trying desperately to hear.

CZERNY AND OTHERS

Beethoven was a very fine teacher, as the great pianist, Carl Czerny, later recalled. He first met the composer in the winter of 1799–1800, when Czerny was ten. He noticed that Beethoven's ears were stuffed with cotton wool on which there was yellow liquid, though his deafness was not yet detectable. Young Czerny was too shy to play Beethoven's music in front of the great man himself, so started with Mozart's C major concerto, with Beethoven himself playing some of the orchestra's music. Czerny particularly noted Beethoven's hairy hands and wide fingers, particularly the tips of them.

As things were going well, Czerny played some newly published Beethoven, the *Pathétique Sonata*, then the song *Adelaide*, which his father sang in his fine tenor voice. 'The boy has talent,' said Beethoven, who decided to take him as a pupil. Czerny would recall how advanced Beethoven's technique was, including the use of the thumb, which was very rare at that time.

He was naturally a demanding teacher, as members of the aristocracy found. Countess Giulietta von Gallenberg looked back in the 1850s to the days when she and some of her friends were his pupils. He accepted no money, but was prepared to take linen that the Countess had sewn. If there were any disturbance, he would walk out. She remembered him as extremely ugly, but also as sensitive, cultured and noble. Usually, he was shabbily dressed.

Czerny was very firm in nailing the lie that Beethoven was oppressed and neglected. In his last years, when his character had been affected by his afflictions, it was not only his loyal friends and patrons who stood by him, but also the ordinary people of Vienna, who, like those of more exalted rank, had come to esteem him. Writing in 1846, Therese von Brunswick recalled him as a stupendous spirit and lamented that her widowed sister had not accepted him as a husband.

Prince Joseph of Liechtenstein and his wife (opposite) were both friends and patrons of Beethoven. Angelica Kauffmann painted this picture of the princess, and that of the prince was painted by J. Lampi the Elder. Both paintings are now in Vaduz castle, the family home.

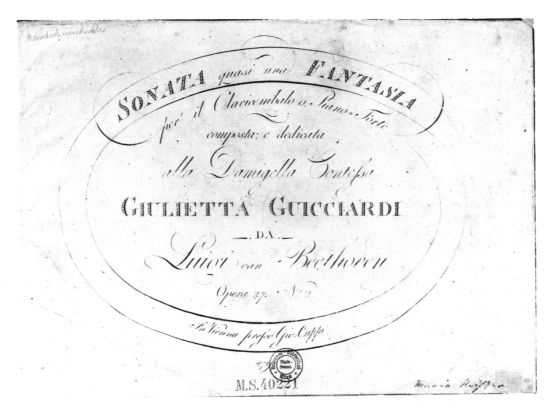

Giulietta
Guicciardi is a
strong contender
for Beethoven's
mysterious
'Immortal
Beloved' – but then
so are many more.
He dedicated his
Moonlight sonata
to her, but
the mystery
remains.

Cipriani Potter, a composer and teacher, left England to meet Beethoven and become his hero's pupil. He has left us a most lively account of the great man.

The English composer, pianist and teacher, Cipriani Potter (1792–1871), was so interested in Beethoven that he went to Vienna and became his pupil in 1818 and 1819. It no doubt helped that Beethoven was an anglophile. Potter, whose fervour is endearing, tended to gush, as fans are wont to do. He described to his hero the effect that his septet had had on him. The great man brushed aside the praise and announced that at that time he had not known how to compose. 'Now,' he said, 'I think I know how to do it.'

Potter had felt rather nervous about approaching the great man, having heard that he was rude and morose. He was also aware that the mere sound of his hero's name had people shaking their heads, and they shook them again when his music was mentioned. Then he met the piano-maker Streicher, who, with his wife Nanette, tried to bring a little order into Beethoven's life.

Left *Aloys Förster
(1748–1823), at
Beethoven's
suggestion agreed
to teach Cipriani
Potter.*

Below *J.G.
Albrechtsberger,
Beethoven's 'old
master', gave the
composer some
lessons in
counterpoint.*

They assured Potter that his fears were unfounded and that Beethoven would be delighted to see him. He set off at once.

He had letters of introduction, one from Dragonetti, the most remarkable double bass player of the day. At once Beethoven became most affable and frank and asked to see some of Potter's work. Potter showed him an overture that he had composed and Beethoven appeared to glance at it somewhat cursorily. The downcast Potter decided that he had looked at it out of sheer politeness but in no detail. So he was amazed when Beethoven picked out a very low note in the bassoon part and told him that it was not a practical one. He made other comments on Potter's work and advised him that he needed a good teacher. He did not teach, and, alas, the man he would have recommended, Albrechtsberger, who had taught him counterpoint, was no longer alive. However, he suggested that he study with Aloys Förster, whom Beethoven regarded as his 'old master.' He did so until the day came when his teacher said that he had studied enough and could concentrate on composing. At once, Beethoven insisted that no-one should give up studying and that he had certainly not studied enough.

Potter clearly wanted to be praised by

Above *There was still plenty of open space around Vienna when Beethoven and Potter took their walks, though not as much as this earlier print suggests.*

Left *The distinguished composer Luigi Cherubini was much admired in Beethoven's day. Born in Italy in 1760, he lived through the age of Mozart and Beethoven and beyond.*

Beethoven to his face. Things reached the point of 'very good' but Potter longed for more. Finally, it came. He also got good advice on an unexpected subject. Beethoven advised him not to compose in a room in which there was a piano, otherwise he would be tempted to head for it. Once the work was completed he could try his music out on it, because there was no certainty that an orchestra would be available.

Potter sometimes walked across the fields with Beethoven to Vienna. He made the most of such occasions. He asked who the greatest living composer was and was told Cherubini. 'And dead composers?' asked Potter. Beethoven said that he had always thought of Mozart as the greatest of all, but since he had come to study Handel, he had decided that Handel was the greatest.

Beethoven was afire to get to England and longed to visit the House of Commons. 'In England you've got your heads on your shoulders,' he stated. Alas, he was never to see his land of heart's desire, though one fears that if he had he might have been disillusioned.

Beethoven was thrilled by the success of Weber's *Der Freischütz* in 1823, not least because the young man was a German composer. He lamented that he no longer went to the theatre. He had not been a great admirer of Weber's music, but he studied the score closely and, in front of friends, praised it to the skies. He had not believed

Beethoven came to believe that the greatest of all composers was Handel. Before, he had rated Mozart supreme.

59

that Weber had it in him to conceive such a masterpiece, and, being Beethoven, made sure that his feelings became known. He embraced Weber fervently when they met. Weber felt that he was being courted by this rough, seemingly unsociable fellow musician. They spent hours together, ate together, and when they parted Weber was, not surprisingly, intoxicated with happi-

A sketch of Beethoven by Josef Böhm.

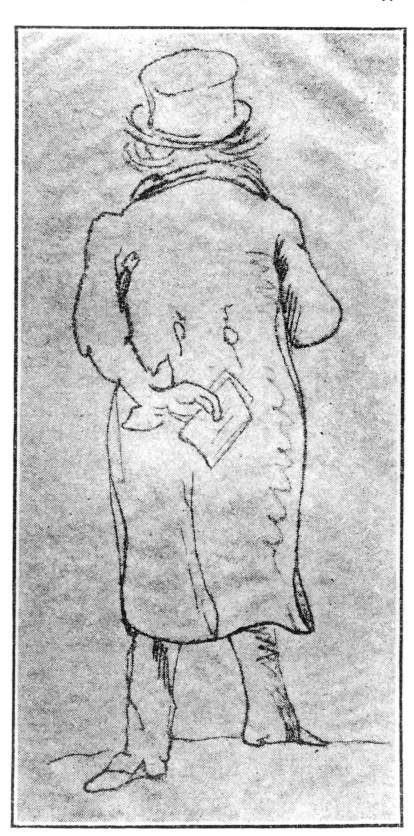

ness. He had seen for himself the state in which Beethoven lived and now he had been privileged to become his friend. He was overwhelmed, and wrote to his wife that he felt exalted.

A LONDON CONNECTION

A most warming account of Beethoven in his last years was written by Johann Andreas Stumpff, a German who had settled in London as a musical instrument maker. On a visit to Vienna he had the opportunity to meet the great man, whom he approached as if he was a supernatural creature, but found that he was very much a human being.

Beethoven was in excellent spirits. 'I'm happy today,' he announced and asked Stumpff how he was liking Vienna, 'where you eat, drink, sleep and –!'

Stumpff was given a very warm welcome and listened to Beethoven extolling the virtues of London and its most cultured inhabitants. In Vienna, so Beethoven believed, all the talk was about food and drink and song and indifferent music. If only Karl could go to England! If he could stay with Stumpff! He asked how much it would cost to keep his nephew in London and made copious notes before launching into a tirade against music publishers. Everything went well and it was arranged that Beethoven would dine with Stumpff in the latter's garden; Stumpff was alerted that Beethoven was devoted to fish dishes. Meanwhile, the joys of London, food included, kept cropping up in the conversation, plus a diatribe against Viennese cooks, then, after verbal swipes at Viennese taste – Rossini rather than Beethoven – all of them delivered with gusto and good humour, it was time for Stumpff to go. He was invited for another visit in three days time.

In fact, Beethoven turned up the next morning and the pair set off for a walk, Beethoven learning how popular his symphonies were in London, the *Pastoral* being the favourite of London ladies. Everyone was looking forward to his Tenth Symphony! Beethoven fervently wished to visit the land where his greatness was appreciated and announced that he would come and stay with his new friend. Before they parted, he pulled some paper out of his breast pocket. Stumpff took it. 'It is meant to represent my face,' said Beethoven, 'though it's not much good and done by an amateur.' Then he looked hard at Stumpff, grabbed his hand, made the paper into a tube and put it to his left ear. Stumpff, speaking very clearly, said: 'If I meet an artist in London to whom I can convey what has left so deep an impression on my soul, I will add those detailed touches that are missing to the finest portrait of yourself. I owe it to your admirers.'

Beethoven embraced Stumpff ecstatically. Just then a funeral procession came towards them. Beethoven slipped away and vanished from Stumpff's sight.

LATE WORKS

In the last few years of his life Beethoven's reputation as a composer was very high indeed, even while his personality seemed eccentric to a degree. The examples given earlier are but a few of his more startling displays. Yet these years saw his most awesome achievements – not only the quartets that have already been noted but three great piano sonatas, radically different from his earlier works, breaking accepted form in the sequence and numbers of movements.

There were also the *Diabelli Variations*, which were based on a waltz by the Austrian composer and publisher, Anton Diabelli.

Fifty composers were commissioned to write a variation apiece on his theme, among them Schubert. Beethoven was invited to participate, but he refused, and proceeded to write 33 variations on the theme. Schubert came up with a delightful variation in the commissioned set; Beethoven's imagination and soaring potency produced a masterpiece.

As far as the average concertgoer is concerned, the towering peak, the great storming

Anton Diabelli was both a publisher and a composer. His waltz, the basis for the Diabelli Variations, *was mocked by Beethoven as a cobbler's patch.*

of music's Valhalla in the early nineteenth century, is the 'Choral' symphony – Beethoven's Ninth in D Minor. Yet the far less often performed *Missa Solemnis*, a stupendous work, is an even more awesome achievement. Both are discussed in the next chapter. The Ninth's origins go back many years, even before Beethoven's first contacts with England in 1803. He had been asked by George Thomson, an Edinburgh publisher, to write sonatas using Scottish melodies, a commission that earned him some easy, steady money. In 1815, his pupil Ferdinand Ries emigrated to London, where he had helped found the Philharmonic Society. The board commissioned three new overtures; none of the three they were sent – *King Stephen*, *Namensfeier* (Name-Day) and *The Ruins of Athens* – was new, as was soon discovered. They also arrived late. It was an unhappy start, which Ries managed to smooth over, but a planned visit to London did not materialize, much to Beethoven's distress. However, his English admirers continued to hope, and to listen to his music, and it was his desire to write a symphony for the Philharmonic Society which was the impetus for his composing the Ninth. In the event, Vienna would hear it before London.

The premiere was on 7 May 1824 and was a financial disaster, even though the work was acclaimed. The mammoth concert also included movements from the *Missa Solemnis* and the stirring overture, *The Consecration of the House*. The performance of the Ninth was a triumph – indeed there was an ovation after the timpani solo in the scherzo, while at the end the composer was turned by one of the soloists, Caroline Unger, to see the audience applauding him. The actual conducting was done by Ignaz Umlauf, who beat time, though Beethoven was, we are told, throwing himself about like a madman. Several musicians present, including the violinist Josef Böhm and the pianist Thalberg, recalled this, and that Beethoven always had to be told – turned – to see the applause.

The *Missa Solemnis* provoked a rare tribute – rare in the old sense of the word – from Prince Golitsïn. After hearing it in St Petersburg he wrote to Beethoven, not simply to tell him that it was a 'treasure trove of beauties' but to say that posterity would pay homage and bless his memory far more than his contemporaries could possibly hope to do.

Ferdinand Ries, like Beethoven, was born in Bonn and became his pupil. Later, he moved to London. A busy conductor, he also wrote eight symphonies and five operas.

ANTON SCHINDLER

N o account of Beethoven can overlook his friend and biographer Anton Schindler (1792–1864), the first of many who put up with a lot for the privilege of being a Boswell. His biography is marred by his wish to present an idealized, santized hero. He went so far as to destroy more than half Beethoven's conversation notebooks, throwing some away because he considered them too mundane for his portrait of a hero. Yet we owe much to Schindler, not least for evidence of Beethoven's warming enthusiasm for the young Schubert's music. Beethoven would cry out that there was a divine spark in Schubert, that he would cause a stir in the world and he lamented that he had not been able to know him earlier.

Again, it is Schindler we have to thank for his description of Beethoven when he was composing the *Missa Solemnis*. The month was August 1819, and Schindler and a musician friend called at Beethoven's house at four o'clock one afternoon. Upon arriv-

Above *One of Beethoven's many dwellings. This house is in Grinzing, Vienna.*

This striking portrait is in Beethoven's birthplace. He was painted a number of times – not surprisingly as his face was full of character.

The ruins of Castle Rauhenstein at Baden, where Beethoven's nephew tried to kill himself.

ing, they found that two of his servant girls had fled that morning after a terrible scene with their master that had occurred some time after midnight . . . .

Both servants had gone to sleep after waiting up for such a long time, while the meal that they had prepared was now uneatable. We heard the master singing behind closed doors in one of his living rooms. He was howling and stamped his foot . . . After some time listening to the dreadful scene, we were all set to go when the door was flung open and Beethoven was there, his face so contorted that one was filled with alarm. He appeared to have endured a life-and-death struggle with the entire tribe of contrapuntalists, who were his perpetual enemies. He started to speak in a confused way, as if he resented our eavesdropping, but presently returned and started speaking of everyday matters, composedly saying: 'A fine state of affairs! Everybody has run away and I

haven't eaten a thing since yesterday noon.' I tried to calm him down and helped him to get dressed. My friend went on ahead to the dining room at the baths so that something could be prepared for our ravenous master. When he got there he lamented the grim state of his household, which was beyond remedy. No work of art of such magnitude can have ever been achieved in more wretched living conditions than the *Missa Solemnis*.

In 1826, a catastrophe occurred. Beethoven had been suffering much anguish from his nephew's behaviour. When Beethoven had brought the subject up, a fierce argument developed which came to a climax, with Karl apparently being hit by his uncle. Karl was now a student at the Technical Institute and examinations were looming. So were his creditors. He decided to kill himself. He purchased two pistols, went to Baden and entered the ruins of Rauhenstein Castle. Climbing to the top of

set off for Vienna in an open carriage, and with him went Karl. He reached Vienna on 2 December and went to bed as soon as he reached his lodgings. He survived what was probably pneumonia only to linger on for some four months with what appeared to be an unknown illness but is now thought to have been cirrhosis of the liver. He was by no means a heavy drinker, but must have been desperately run down.

In increasing pain, and with nurses who allowed him to become verminous, he was tapped for dropsy. He also had jaundice. Yet these days were not without comfort. From Johann Stumpff, his London friend, came a large edition of Handel. He read the proofs of the *Choral Symphony* and wrote to the London Philharmonic Society, thanking them for £100 that they had sent him. He assured them that they would receive his Tenth Symphony. Some Schubert songs gave him much pleasure. On 24 March 1827, he was given the last rites of the Catholic Church, those with him including his brother Johann and his wife, Schindler, and the young son of his friend Gerhard von Breuning, who ran errands and cheered Beethoven up.

On the afternoon of 26 March 1827, a sister-in-law of Beethoven and Schubert's friend Hüttenbrenner were alone with the dying man. Suddenly there was a flash of

the tower, he held the pistol to his forehead and fired, managing only superficial wounds. He was taken to his mother's house in Vienna. It was the final climax in a sad story of over-possessive love.

Karl's entry in one of Beethoven's conversation books is a pitiful but deeply felt apology. He swore that he would never get drunk again: he had been drunk, he wrote, when it happened. Abjectly, he begged for forgiveness. It was decided that the youth should enter the Army after convalescing in the country. Both Beethoven and Karl would stay near Vienna with the composer's brother Johann, who was a successful chemist.

THE LAST MONTHS

Once again, tensions mounted. Beethoven was concerned about Karl and had always been deeply suspicious of his sister-in-law. In severe winter weather he

Stephan von Breuning, one of the aristocrats who tried to organize the composer's life, a hopeless task

lightning which lit up the room, and a thunderclap, Beethoven opened his eyes, raised his right hand and, with a clenched fist, looked up for some seconds, his face serious and threatening. Moments later, he was dead.

Three days later, on 29 March 1827, he was buried in the Währing cemetery. Vienna gave him a farewell that Royalty might envy, some 10,000 people being present. Priests, poets, actors, singers and musicians were there and Beethoven's

Equali for All Souls' Day, arranged for voices, was played. After the church ceremony was over, all moved towards the church of the Minories. An actor spoke a funeral oration at the cemetery gates and soon the coffin was being laid silently into

Above *Beethoven's grave in Vienna, beside those of other great musicians, among them Brahms, Schubert and Wolf.*

Left *An artist's impression of the magnificent funeral procession accorded to Beethoven. Different sources state that between 10,000 and 20,000 were present.*

the grave. He was 56 years old.

One person that day had no idea what was happening and asked an old woman what was going on. 'They are burying the general of the musicians,' she replied. Today he lies with other musicians in the Central Friedhof. There is nothing like it anywhere else, for there in a small space are the graves of Brahms, Schubert, Gluck, Suppé, Hugo Wolf and Johann Strauss, as well as a cenotaph commemorating Mozart. And there, too, lies Beethoven.

Beethoven, the liberator, set off an explosive era which transformed music as a whole, not just German music. As Peter Heyworth has noted, composers as different as Berlioz and Bartok, Tchaikovsky and Bruckner, all felt the force of his example. He more than anyone gave the composer the chance to force listeners to recognize a musician's character, the character with which the genius proclaims his identity.

We must know in our hearts that his final period, cut off as he was so cruelly from others, benefitted us, for to survive he had to fight, to compose, to endure.

Proof of his extraordinary success is twofold. Firstly, in his third period he made a voyage into the music of the future more questing and bold than anything achieved by later composers. His was the very opposite of the society founded by Schoenberg in 1919 – a Society for Private Performance, which barred ordinary listeners from attending. Beethoven had a different, all-embracing vision, as his last symphony proclaims. 'O friends', the soloist sings – to the world, to Beethoven's world, to ours.

Franz Grillparzer, the Austrian poet and playwright, wrote Beethoven's funeral oration, a most moving one, ending with the words: 'and when he died we wept'.

Einladung

zu

Ludwig van Beethoven's

Leichenbegängniss,

welches am 29. März um 3 Uhr Nachmittags Statt finden wird.

Man versammelt sich in der Wohnung des Verstorbenen im Schwarzspanier-Hause Nr. 200, am Glacis vor dem Schottenthore.

Der Zug begibt sich von da nach der Dreyfaltigkeits-Kirche bey den P. P. Minoriten in der Alsergasse.

Die musikalische Welt erlitt den unersetzlichen Verlust des berühmten Tondichters am 26. März 1827 Abends gegen 6 Uhr. Beethoven starb an den Folgen der Wassersucht, im 56. Jahre seines Alters, nach empfangenen heil. Sacramenten,

Der Tag der Exequien wird nachträglich bekannt gemacht von

L. van Beethoven's
Verehrern und Freunden.

(Diese Karte wird in Tob. Haslingers Musikhandlung vertheilt.)   Gedruckt bey Anton Strauss.

Above *The invitation to Beethoven's funeral.*

Left *Beethoven's death mask by Joseph Danhauser. Some dislike it, but others believe it catches Beethoven's greatness.*

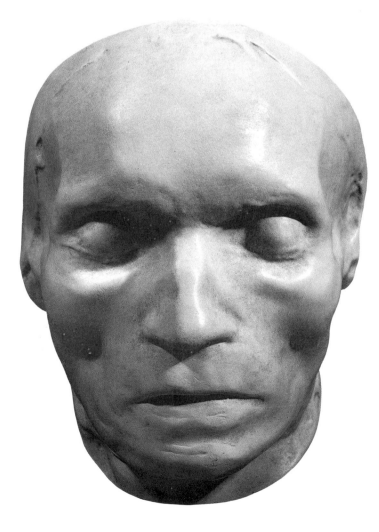

BEETHOVEN'S MUSIC

Beethoven's music, though rooted firmly in the classical tradition of Haydn and Mozart, also anticipated the Romantic movement personified by Schubert and Schumann.

The current edition of Grove's monumental *Dictionary of Music and Musicians* has an entry on Beethoven that is the length of a fair-sized book. Its first paragraph carefully states that he is 'probably the most admired composer in the history of Western music.' Equally magisterial is the statement in Scholes' *The Oxford Companion to Music* that 'more than any composer he deserves to be called the Shakespeare of music.'

Though a classical composer like Haydn and Mozart, Beethoven paved the way for the Romantic Movement in music. He was the standard-bearer for Schubert and his successors down to Mahler and Richard Strauss.

Only the tone deaf and the culturally deprived can go through life without being aware of the Fifth Symphony, whose opening notes were a rallying cry to supporters of the Allies over the radio in occupied Europe during the Second World War. And Beethoven's deafness is surely known to millions who have only a modicum of general knowledge. He above all other composers spells great music to the mythical man and woman in the street, music-lover or not. His music is

for all seasons. Beethoven was a colossus and will remain one as long as music endures.

When his opera *Fidelio* was being rehearsed, he found that there were only two bassoonists present, not three. Prince Franz Joseph Lobkowitz, a patron and a friend of

Opposite *The statue of Beethoven which stands in his birthplace, Bonn.*

Left *Wolfgang Amadeus Mozart (1756–91). After hearing Beethoven play he told his friends: 'Keep your eyes on that fellow.'*

Franz Schubert (1797–1828) impressed Beethoven, who was delighted with the number of fine songs that the young man had composed.

Igor Stravinsky was at one time among a minority who have disliked Beethoven's music, but later he recanted.

A page from the manuscript of the Appassionata *sonata.*

the composer, suggested that two would suffice. Despite his commitments, Beethoven brooded about the prince's remark and that night stormed his palace. He reached the bottom of the staircase and then seemed to explode. He roared: 'You idiot! You idiot!'

Only between the wars has Beethoven's music been seriously questioned, indeed sometimes savaged, by a small group of composers, notably Stravinsky, Satie and Hindemith, though there are others, among them Benjamin Britten, who, having loved him, turned against him. The other composers and their lesser-known supporters were described by the critic Peter Heyworth in 1980. These composer-critics reproached him, wrote Heyworth, for 'his seriousness, his assertiveness, his loudness, his tendency to what they considered moralizing rhetoric,' indeed for virtually everything that had come after him. Later, the great Stravinsky recanted. As Heyworth noted, to blame Beethoven for the misdeeds and failings of romanticism during the extrordinary musical expansion of the nineteenth century is about as intelligent as to make Bismarck responsible for the misdeeds of Adolf Hitler.

The student of Beethoven's life, especially his early life, discovers many contradictions, not least about his boyhood. He was at once very unhappy and a contented youth – his family life was happy by some accounts and deeply unhappy by others. Fortunately, fascinating as Beethoven's life is, what matters is his music, the joy and consolation of millions of his fellow human beings.

Beethoven was a prodigious worker, which was just as well for his millions of admirers. For him, unlike Mozart and Schubert, composing was, so it seems, always hard work. It would be wrong to suggest that composition was always easy for Mozart, but Beethoven wielded a broadsword, Mozart a rapier. Everest was always Beethoven's goal in his grandest works. Mozart was content with the many splendours of the Alps.

In his attitude to life and his art, Beethoven was like Tennyson's Ulysses, who was determined to go on though

Made weak by time and fate, but strong in will
To strive, to seek, to find, and not to yield.

That will produced nine symphonies; seven concertos, five of them for piano, one for violin and one a triple concerto for piano, violin and cello; 32 piano sonatas; five sonatas for piano and cello and ten for piano and violin; the great Mass in D and the Mass in C; *Fidelio*; five string trios and seven piano trios; a septet for string and wind, and a piano and wind quintet; incidental music for plays, the most famous being the *Egmont* overture and the even greater overture to *Coriolan*. There were also concert overtures, a wealth of small-scale piano music, cantatas and songs (including the first song-cycle) along with bagatelles, rondos and variations, also a *Choral Fantasy*.

There follows a more detailed account of a small number of Beethoven's works, a representative selection but a mighty handful of his output. The dates at the head of each

entry refer to the year or years of the work's composition. The Fifth Symphony is omitted despite its shift in emphasis to make the finale the climax of the symphony, for it is the opening movement of the *Eroica* which must surely remain the greatest step forward.

PIANO CONCERTO Number Four in G, Opus 58: 1800–01(?)

No concerto has a more beguilingly beautiful opening than Beethoven's Fourth. It is like none of his others, for the piano states the chief subject, a delicate one of great beauty, at the very start. A long and quietly joyous passage stems from it in the orchestra, which grows in power. The second subject adds to the emotional feeling until at last the piano returns. There are bravura chromatic scale passages, yet everything has grown from the opening bars, and these bars continue to influence the unique atmosphere of this much-loved masterpiece. There is infinite variety in this extraordinary movement.

The second movement has been famously described by Liszt as a representation of Orpheus taming the Furies. Basil Deane states that its poignancy is unique and quite indescribable. It presents no problems, even

Daniel Barenboim, a fine interpreter of Beethoven's music, with an instrument of a power unknown to the composer.

75

Rodolphe Kreutzer (1766–1831) was a prolific composer and a very fine violinist. Beethoven dedicated to him a magnificent sonata for piano and violin, which bears his name.

at first hearing.

The last movement, delicate and explosive, is endlessly inventive. Beethoven issued an order to future players: the cadenza in the last movement was to be short. He did not want his perfectly judged structure to be harmed by vanity. Almost at the end a tender passage turns to exhilarating, headlong speed, and the miraculous work is over. *First performance:* March 1807

SONATA Number Nine in A major for Violin and Piano, Opus 47, 'Kreutzer': 1803

An unusual visitor to Vienna in 1803 was George Polgreen Bridgetower, who was the mulatto son of Prince Nicolaus Esterházy's page August. Beethoven wrote the sonata

for Bridgetower, but the pair fell out over a woman and Rodolphe Kreutzer received the dedication instead. The original dedication deserves quoting, however: 'Mulattick Sonata. Composed for the mulatto Brischdauer, great lunatik and mulattick composer.' For further information about him Betty Matthews' article, 'George Polgreen Bridgetower' in *The Music Review*, February 1968, can be consulted.

The *Kreutzer* is considered by many to be the finest sonata composed up to that time, a work for the concert hall rather than the home, at a time when Vienna was becoming used to public concerts. The first movement, splendid and deeply moving, stands alone in many opinions. Its peak is reached in a magnificent last theme that reigns over the development section of the movement.

There follow magnificent variations on a

graceful theme, though the heights of the first movement do not carry over to the second. The last movement was originally the finale of the Sonata in A, Opus 30. It is not really a suitable ending. Marion Scott summed up the situation brilliantly when she wrote that it is as if, having begun as Othello and Desdemona, the characters suddenly turn into Figaro and Susanna, a less than ideal transplant.
First performance: 1803

SYMPHONY *Number Three in E Flat Major,*
'Eroica': 1803–04

It used to be the fashion to find messages in Beethoven, notably in the scherzo of the *Eroica*. It was 'found' to be an excited crowd awaiting their hero, who speaks to them in the trio, or a fickle crowd who will desert him, or spring after winter, or other such tosh. Yet all we really need to know – and for those who wish to know more, Chapter Eleven of Marion Scott's biography will tell them more – is that Beethoven had hero-worshipped Bonaparte, but was totally alienated when he became the Emperor Napoleon. He had dedicated this great symphony to a republican hero, but now he tore off the dedication. The non-dedication reads (in Italian): 'Heroic Symphony, composed to celebrate the memory of a great man.' The great man was still alive but, as far as Beethoven was concerned, his greatness had departed.

Meanwhile, the music lives on as one of Beethoven's supreme masterpieces, which changed the course of musical history. The

Lobkowitz Palace in Vienna was the home of Prince Franz Lobkowitz, whose children Beethoven taught for a time. The Eroica *Symphony is dedicated to him.*

The young Napoleon painted against an Italian background: the image of the liberator and conqueror of Beethoven's dreams – which would be shattered.

giant step forward at the very opening is a revolution in itself, totally different from any other music ever written, always astounding whenever it is heard, as is the rest of the movement. The revolution continues, through the ultimate funeral march, only equalled by Siegfried's Funeral March in *Götterdämmerung*. The scintillating scherzo is the composer's first large-scale development of a third movement, light years ahead of stately minuets, while the romantically introduced horn calls in the trio add sheer magic to the music. The finale is a theme and variations worthy of what has gone before. Beethoven had used the theme before, three times indeed! From it springs a finale as inventive as it is profound. There followed the vivacious and serious Fourth Symphony, then the Fifth, which would establish the last movement as the climax of the symphonic form.
First performance: 7 April 1805

FIDELIO:
1805/1806/1814

Beethoven's high ideals saw to it that opera played only a minor role in his career. Though he could worship Mozart the musi-

cian, he lamented his choice of subjects. He found *Don Giovanni* and even *The Marriage of Figaro* 'repugnant' and 'too frivolous.' *The Magic Flute* naturally appealed to him more.

Beethoven strove mightily with many of his works, but with none more so than *Fidelio*. Being Beethoven, he produced a masterpiece, which, unless disastrously performed, is always a major musical and emotional occasion. The story is based on a true incident of the French Revolution, when a wife dressed herself as a man to rescue her husband, a political prisoner in France during the Reign of Terror. The plot of the opera, a good melodramatic one, stirred Beethoven deeply. It begins as a *singspiel* (with dialogue) and ends as a sublime masterpiece, a genuine and deeply emotional music drama.

The light opening does nothing to indicate that a peak of emotion will be reached in the first act. We have the disguised heroine Leonore causing Marzelline, jailer Rocco's daughter, to fall in love with 'him' while Leonore's mind is on finding and rescuing her husband, Florestan. Florestan's enemy, the villainous governor Pizarro, wants him dead. Leonore is calling herself Fidelio.

Pizarro reaches the prison and gives vent

78

Wilhelmine Schröder-Devrient (1804–60), was one of the greatest actress-singers in the history of opera. Her Leonore in Beethoven's Fidelio *is a legend to this day.*

The French Revolution affected the arts as well as politics. The killing of a king and the Reign of Terror that followed made for a turbulent era. Against this background Beethoven made his incomparable mark on music.

79

to his delight that Florestan will soon be dead. A shocked Rocco is told that Florestan must be killed. Leonore's great aria 'Abscheulicher' charts her hopes and fears, before 'Fidelio' persuades Rocco to allow the prisoners a short respite in the castle gardens. There follows the great and noble Prisoners' Chorus, a cry of hope as apt and stirring today as it was in Beethoven's day. Pizarro appears and the prisoners are entombed again.

Act Two is set in the dungeon where Florestan is imprisoned. If Beethoven had written nothing else, this scene would indicate what opera had lost. Florestan, in chains, sings – lives – his despair, then has a vision of an angel like his Leonore. He falls down exhausted. Into the dungeon descends Rocco – with Leonore, who has persuaded him to let her help him dig a grave. Even though she is aware that the prisoner might *not* be her husband, she is determined to save him.

Florestan wakes and Leonore recognizes him and faints. Floreston learns that it is his enemy Pizarro who has imprisoned him and asks that his wife be sent for. It is impossible, says Rocco. Soon Pizarro arrives. He delights in telling Florestan who his murderer is before killing him, but, as he approaches, Leonore shrieks 'Back!' and

shields Florestan with her body. She reveals who she is and with ever-mounting tension the climax comes. Pizarro prepares to kill both husband and wife, but Leonore produces a pistol and says she will shoot him – and just at that moment a trumpet call sounds out: the Minister has arrived, and he will bring justice. Beethoven has lifted an excellent melodramatic scene of song and of speech to the height of drama.

Finally Florestan asks Leonore wonderingly what she has suffered. Speaking, not singing, she replies 'Nothing, my Florestan!' The scene ends with a duet of sheerest rapture.

The Minister, Don Fernando, is ready and the scene changes to the castle's parade ground. Beethoven achieves miracles of pacing so that climax after climax of joy never flag into mere repetition, and a supreme moment of emotion occurs when Florestan's chains are removed by his Leonore. Pizarro apart, only Marzelline has cause to lament, having discovered that her beloved is a woman. The sound of this final scene is martial and exuberant.

Even allowing for the fact that the earlier versions of *Fidelio/Leonore* were not very satisfactory compared with *Fidelio*, the barrage of criticism levelled at it seems to have been excessive. It is true that the 1805

The Theater an der Wien opened in 1801, and in 1805 Fidelio was staged there. The opera had undergone a number of changes, musical and structural, but remains a blazing masterpiece of great intensity and feeling.

Anna Mildner-Hauptmann as Leonore in Beethoven's Fidelio. *She was the first to sing the great role. She had an immense voice – 'Like a house,' according to Haydn. Alas, she was no actress.*

cast was below standard, with the men leaving much to be desired, though the women were better. Yet *Fidelio* seemed to be destined for success. It was considered a trump card.

But the war was heading for Vienna – and a week before Fidelio's opening night, the French arrived. The Court and its inhabitants had fled, those who could, and the streets were full of French soldiers, on their best behaviour it seems. But with food stocks being low and with fears of possible trouble in the streets, theatre business was bad. The French officers at least were eager for a night at the opera, though some who would have liked to go were too busy trying to cope with the political situation. *Fidelio* was compared unfavourably with Mozart's operas, also Cherubini's, and was dropped after three performances.

However, with some kind of normality being restored under the French occupa-

tion, the aristocrats and music-lovers returned to Vienna. There was pressure for a revival, but it was felt that Beethoven must agree to drastic cuts.

Many of Beethoven's friends and supporters had now gathered including the playwright von Collin, author of *Coriolan*, Beethoven's brother Caspar, Stefan von Breuning, and other able and noted members of Vienna's artistic fraternity. Röckl, the Florestan, had only recently arrived in the capital and now he found himself meeting Beethoven. The assembled gathering decided to take the opera apart and put it together again, a process not unknown today in theatrical circles, though now there would be a less aristocratic gathering in action. It was decided that the whole work must be gone through; everyone considered it a worthwhile exercise. Prince Lichnowsky was at the piano, looking at the orchestral score, and Clemento proceeded to accompany the entire opera on his violin – from memory. He was well known for his amazing memory and those present took it for granted.

Beethoven was understandably in a fury, and it was a ferocious one even by his standards. Fortunately, Princess Lichnowsky was a most sympathetic person, indeed, a second mother to him, and because of her tact and influence something at least got done. After six hours, Beethoven was persuaded to cut three numbers from the first act. All those who have been in the world of the theatre will recognize the truth of this story. And there is a postscript to it. At last the truly battered assembly started to eat, and now Beethoven, clearly the professional who knew when to stop fighting, was the happiest person, so it would seem, in the room. He saw his Florestan, Joseph Röckl, and asked what he was eating. Röckl confessed that he did not know. This mightily amused Beethoven, who roared: 'He eats like a wolf, but doesn't know what!' It was clearly a high spot of his gruelling day.

Beethoven's Fidelio *is rarely out of the repertoire of the world's opera houses, including Covent Garden. Pictured here are Elizabeth Connell as Leonore and Klaus König as Florestan in one of the most famous scenes in all opera.*

First performance: 1805
First performance final version: 23 May 1814

A footnote is needed to indicate something of the opera's somewhat traumatic history. It is a German version of 'Leonore, ou L'amour Conjugal', originally set to music by Gaveaux in 1798, then by Paer in an Italian version in 1804 and Mayr in 1805. Originally in three acts, the libretto was cut to two acts in 1806 by Stefan von Breuning. Its final form dates from 1814, the work of Georg Friedrich Treitschke. Vienna saw the first version at the Theater an der Wien on 20 November 1805. On 29 March 1806 the second version was given at the same theatre, while the third version was staged at the Kärntnertor-Theater on 23 May 1814. London first saw it in 1832, New York in 1839.

Beethoven tried three versions of the overture (known as *Leonore* overtures numbers 1, 2 and 3) before the one normally heard now, the *Fidelio* overture. Until quite

recently, Leonore number 3 was regularly included between the last two scenes by scores of conductors, great and not so great, although it wilfully holds up the drama at a critical point.

VIOLIN CONCERTO in D, Opus 61: 1806

Beethoven's was the first great violin concerto. His Romances for Violin and Orchestra are pleasant pieces, while his Triple Concerto is merely adequate by his own high standards. The Violin Concerto, however, is one of his supreme masterpieces. Mendelssohn's is more scintillating, a bravura showpiece, but it inhabits a lower level of inspiration. The Brahms Concerto, in the Beethoven mould, is a glorious, much loved work. Yet Beethoven's apparently simpler concerto inhabits a serene plateau of inspiration that makes it unique. For some, the four drum beats that start the concerto so memorably sound slightly sinister. For others, they are mysterious.

After the opening there is a long, stirring and beautiful sequence for the orchestra, classical, simple and tender. The second

subject, emotional as it is, is also sublimely simple. The premiere in 1806 got the work off to a bad start because the great Clemento had to sight-read it.

Above *The final scene of* Fidelio, *one of the most exhilaratingly glorious ever conceived. On the left Jon Vickers as Florestan with Linda Esther Gray as Leonore.*

Left *Josef Joachim, the most popular violinist of his age. This Austro-Hungarian virtuoso was a famous exponent of the Beethoven concerto and his cadenzas for the work are frequently used. He died in Berlin in 1907.*

As in all Beethoven's concertos, the soloist is the dominant figure, a new development in music. Listen for the famous moment which occurs just before the recapitulation, a moment which the great Joachim played so wonderfully that his hearers never forgot it. The beautifully scored slow movement is as ethereal as any music Beethoven wrote, while the last movement, a rondo, brings the masterly concerto to a stimulating conclusion.
First performance: 1806

Overture CORIOLANUS,
Opus 62: 1807

This magnificently powerful overture was not inspired by Shakespeare's *Coriolanus*, though its starkly vivid music is worthy of the supreme dramatist. Indeed, only Shakespeare could follow such a titanic opening.

Heinrich Joseph von Collin was no Shake-

speare, but he wrote a number of verse plays on classical themes. His short life was lived in a period of almost constant warfare. Beethoven was inspired by his friend's work to write a masterpiece, which ranks as his finest overture. Only one theme reflects deep emotion, presumably that of Virgilia, Coriolanus' wife. It could hardly reflect the character of the anti-hero's bloodthirsty mother Volumnia.

The violence of the music, concentrated and savage, is unique in Beethoven's work. If none of Beethoven's music survived except this, musicians and audiences alike would be aware of an exceptional talent.
First performance: 1807

PIANO CONCERTO Number Five in E Flat,
Opus 73, 'The Emperor': 1809

Beethoven's fifth and final piano concerto

This piano was given to Beethoven by Nanette von Streicher, the daughter of the noted piano-maker, Johann Andreas Stein.

dates from 1809. On the journey from his so-called Second Piano Concerto, written before his official first and sounding it, he had progressed steadily and gloriously. The perfection of the Fourth Concerto has been noted, and the very different Fifth cannot be left out even from a short list. In their different ways they are twin peaks of his achievement.

The name *Emperor* was not Beethoven's, though it is a perfectly valid one, even though his old hero, Bonaparte, had betrayed him by becoming the Emperor Napoleon. That the first and last movements are heroic as well as beautiful can hardly be challenged. Great arpeggio chords at the start usher in a theme of stirring and melodic power, and the second subject, hauntingly helped by the composer's inspirational use of horns, adds to its dramatic beauty. In partnership with the orchestra, the piano is by turns heart-lifting, magical, delicate and powerful.

The haunting second movement starts quietly with a long, slow theme, and the piano quietly joins the orchestra in a subject of limpid beauty exceptional even for Beethoven. The most famous coup comes at the movement's close when Beethoven comes down from B natural to B flat, a moment of witchcraft; then the rondo starts, exceptionally exhilarating and inventive. Just before the end the tempo slows down. A drum accompanies the piano. There is a flourish on the piano, a farewell from the orchestra and the *Emperor* is over.
First performance: 1809

Most of the greatest modern pianists have recorded the Fourth and Fifth concertos on at least one occasion, and it is fascinating to observe the subtle differences in the interpretations of acknowledged masters such as Wilhelm Kempff, Rudolf Serkin, Emil Gilels, Claudio Arrau, Alfred Brendel and Vladimir Ashkenazy.

Baroness Dorothea von Ertmann is another possible candidate for Beethoven's 'Immortal Beloved'. She was certainly a very fine pianist.

TRIO in B Flat Major, Opus 97, 'Archduke': 1811

This trio is one of Beethoven's most popular works, as well as being a masterpiece. The unblessed who feel that chamber music is not for them could well be converted to it through listening to its first movement. Chamber music is a friendly activity, an intimate form of art, and this is an ideal introduction.

It was composed in March 1811, after some preliminary sketches the year before. No doubt it was played privately soon after, but it was first performed publicly on 11 April 1814, with a splendid trio led by Schuppanzigh, with Linke as the cellist and Beethoven at the piano.

It was one of Beethoven's last appearances at the piano, and seems to have been a near shambles. Spohr was one of those who was deeply distressed, as was Ignaz Moscheles, himself a composer and pianist. The latter had no doubts about the music. He noted that many works were said to be new, but Beethoven's really were, for they were truly original.

After the first movement there is a delicate and delightful scherzo, the following trio being slightly weightier, then we return to the scherzo. The music is gossamer light, but, as so often with Beethoven, deeply felt.

There follows a glorious third movement, quietly passionate. (Years later, Franz Liszt, not content to leave a masterpiece alone, decided to orchestrate it to start his *Cantata for the Beethoven Centennial Celebration*, which was heard on 29 May 1870.) The masterpiece ends with a brisk, cheerful rondo, shadowed by more sombre passages that recall the mood of the slow movement. It is a very much loved work.
First performance: 1814

SYMPHONY Number Seven in A Major, Opus 92: 1811–12

Wagner called Beethoven's Seventh Symphony 'the apotheosis of the dance', indeed on one occasion in Venice Wagner danced to it, accompanied by Liszt. It was completed in 1812 and was first performed on 8 December 1813 at the famous charity concert for those wounded in the Battle of Hanau, along with *Wellington's Victory, or The Battle of Vitoria*. The pot-boiler was a huge success, but so was the new symphony, the sensible Viennese being able to enjoy both.

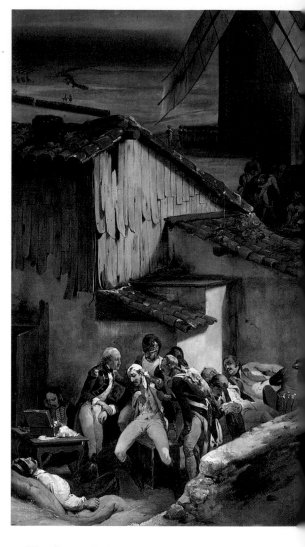

The Seventh begins with an impressive, slow introduction, then the woodwind ushers in one of the most ravishing themes in the symphonies, which the orchestra takes up. The second subject is in the same exhilarating vein, and the development keeps up the momentum. After the vigorously exuberant recapitulation, the music moves towards sheer exaltation, an apotheosis indeed. Few codas, even in Beethoven, reach such dizzy, joyous heights, complete with music for horns which must have taxed the players of the instruments of that time.

The second movement, one of Beethoven's most famous and inspiring conceptions, and gravely beautiful, is marked *Allegretto* and has delighted audiences since first heard in Vienna. It is simple and stately. The scherzo's exuberance is beautifully contrasted with a trio of dignified charm that builds up to an impressive climax. The finale is happily described by Gordon Jacob as a 'veritable bacchic orgy' contained within the confines of sonata form. The symphony's popularity has always been immense.
First performance: 8 December 1813

The Battle of Valmy was fought in 1792, Beethoven's friend Goethe being present. The Prussians were routed. Beethoven was not a soldier, but he played a notable role in the new age, even though he later lost faith in Napoleon.

Richard Wagner (1813–83) was one of Beethoven's musical heirs. He coined the famous phrase, 'the apotheosis of the dance,' to describe the last movement of the Seventh Symphony.

MASS in D,
Opus 123, 'Missa Solemnis': 1819–23

Considering that it is one of the most dramatic, vast and inspirational works ever conceived and executed, Beethoven's *Missa Solemnis* is not very well-known. The reason can only be that it is ferociously difficult to sing, with all the necessary extra rehearsals that that involves.

As Anthony Lewis has explained in the Choral Music section of *The Age of Beethoven*, Beethoven's imagination could be fired by such a text, but not restricted by it. The result is a unique work of art, his own statement on the Mass, with his creative urge at white heat. Miraculously, for all its musical depth, it can overwhelm the listener even at first hearing.

Professor Lewis has explained how 'the intricate subjective polyphony of Bach, in which each voice seems to be uttering a personal statement on the text' is joined to 'the more homophonic textures and clearer rhythms of Italian eighteenth century choral music.' Beethoven was genius enough to achieve what Professor Lewis has called stylistic integration. It is endlessly exciting –

and sublime experience for listeners.

As recently as 1938, Walter Reizler in his biography of Beethoven could worry about the composer's Catholicism having been called into question. Today, believers and non-believers alike would surely consider such comments risible.

After a brief orchestral opening of stateliness and feeling, 'Kyrie' rings out and a great edifice of sound is built up. This is strong, emotionally charged music, then, with the *Gloria*, there is one of the most thrilling outbursts of praise in music. After a powerful fugal passage, there is a virtual shout of 'Glorificamus.' The *Qui tollis* is a lovely one with expressive use of words, while after a giant fugue and other marvels, the section ends with three exciting, almost frenzied, overwhelming vocal fanfares of 'Gloria!'

The *Credo* is on an even vaster scale than the *Gloria*, the choir repeating the word time and again. 'Et incarnatus' is a most beautiful section, where, as William Mann has noted, the orchestra seems to depict the Cross being held aloft. The tragedy of the Passion is most beautifully evoked, then the Resurrection – 'Resurrexit.' There is a fugal

Johann Sebastian Bach (1685–1750), one of the greatest founding fathers of German music, who influenced those who followed him, including Beethoven.

Opposite
Beethoven's house in Mödling, where he worked on the Missa Solemnis. *His rooms – wherever he was – tended to be chaotic.*

ending to the movement, dry words to portray the vast structure that carries it to its monumental end.

The *Sanctus* begins quietly and solemnly, unlike Bach's, Mozart's or Verdi's. It is holy music indeed. Then majestic uproar bursts forth as the heavens open. A most beautiful *Praeludium* is heard, with flutes, bassoons and strings accompanying. When the bread and the wine are made into the Body and Blood of Christ, Beethoven begins one of his most beautiful passages, the equivalent of a slow movement of a violin concerto – the *Benedictus*. The choir sings 'Osanna' again, the violin plays the truly heavenly obbligato once more. The miracle is over.

There follows the *Agnus Dei*, a dark section, a *miserere* of the most solemn hue, but now other voices are heard repeating the prayer three times. Beethoven subtly lightens the mood, but not for long. Martial music is heard in the distance, trumpets and drum stir memories of war, or threats of it. The passages are heard more than once and cast a shadow as topical today as it was then. There is no comfortable end to this towering work. Even at the last, drum beats can be heard, but at the very end there is peace – perhaps . . .

First performance: 1824

NINTH SYMPHONY in D Minor, 'Choral': 1817–18 and 1822–24

Beethoven's Eighth Symphony had been the shortest of his symphonies, a good-humoured affair with a throwback to the past, a minuet for the third movement, not a scherzo. Only bores, then as now, objected, especially contemporaries who expected profundity and the sublime at all times. In the event, they were to get with the Ninth what they and most music lovers wanted, an epic symphony, whose last movement divides opinions to this day.

It behoves the author to confess that his first experience of the Ninth – at the Royal Albert Hall not long after the Second World War ended – was one of the experiences of a lifetime. It came at the end of a cycle of Beethoven's symphonies conducted by Victor de Sabata, a musician whom many regarded as even finer than Toscanini in the opera house and concert hall.

Love and brotherhood and sisterhood are the themes of the last great movement, a vision of a Utopian world. This setting of Schiller's *Ode to Joy* has detractors of its music, though Martin Cooper has reminded us that Schiller was not apostrophizing joy (Freude) but freedom (Freiheit), not the

Otto Klemperer (1885–1973) is widely regarded as one of the greatest of all conductors of Beethoven's music. Happily, records exist to prove his greatness.

90

most popular theme at the time of the French Revolution.

The opening movement has attracted a Niagara of comment. By its very nature, by the sheer daring of its giant stride into the future, one can understand why Marion Scott felt that Beethoven had taken us with him to 'inter-stellar spaces.' This is tough, swirling, forceful music. It sent Wagner into ecstasies. And if the Seventh Symphony is the apotheosis of the dance, then what is the giant scherzo of the Ninth? The trio is Breughel-like and energetic, military but not militaristic. There are extraordinary drum passages and explosions of sound.

The slow movement, said Parry, is the finest orchestral example of a theme and variations. In fact, there are two different themes, one hymn-like, the other an exquisite, tender passage, the two themes changing characters, or so it appears. Then fanfares introduce the coda which flows

Friedrich Schiller (1759–1805), one of Europe's greatest dramatists and poets, was the source of many opera plots, notably Don Carlo.

91

Above *Sir George Smart (1776–1867), the notable conductor, was a friend of Beethoven.*

away with quiet beauty.

Now comes the start of the great choral movement, though the choir does not start it. A tremendous drama occurs, featuring glimpses of the earlier movements. All are dismissed and we get the first glimpse of what is to be, first in the cellos and basses, then through the rest of the orchestra. One of the most famous of all melodies is born, made even more memorable by supporting counter-melodies. The full orchestra takes up the great hymn, a wordless one as yet. Then all dissolves in chaos. Now Beethoven demands the intercession of the human voice. 'O friends,' sings the baritone soloist, 'not these sounds, but more pleasant ones, full of gladness.' The words are Beethoven's own. The baritone starts the ode, which the chorus takes up. The tenor sings a rousing march section, and a vigorous orchestral interlude follows. Universal brotherhood is called for. A thrilling chorus of two simultaneous themes; the soloists have a final moment, the chorus joins in with them in an ecstatic lyrical passage, then a veritable explosion of sound erupts, calmed once more by a lyric passage, then, in a prestissimo flood of rejoicing, the Ninth Symphony ends with unconfined joy indeed.

First performance: 17 May 1824

QUARTET in E Flat Major, Opus 127: 1823–24

Beethoven finished this powerful and beautiful quartet in late 1824. It was the first of those five quartets which broke the mould of quartet form and are for many both his last and his greatest masterpieces. It is also a wonderful farewell to his immediate past, a

*Otto Klemperer
rehearsing for a
performance of
Beethoven's Choral
Symphony.*

masterpiece to inspire even the most timid Beethoven lover who believes that chamber music is somehow less accessible than other kinds. For this is a work at once profound yet instantly appealing.

It begins with a brief but striking prelude, which will be heard twice more in different keys, then a flood of melody, beautiful and soothing. Next comes a sublime slow move-ment of exquisite feeling and emotion.

There follows a long and fascinating scherzo, with startling changes of tempo and equally startling surprises. The final move-ment teems with life, abounds in good tunes and good humour, sometimes uproarious, sometimes mellow. Suddenly and unexpect-edly, it is over. The great magician knew the moment to stop.

INDEX

PICTURE ACKNOWLEDGMENTS

The painting on page 44 (top) is reproduced by gracious permission of Her Majesty The Queen.

Archiv für Kunst und Geschichte 7 bottom, 81; Clive Barda 82, 83 top; Barnaby's Picture Library 67; Bavaria-Verlag Bildagentur/atpo Wien 46–47, A. Gruber 35 top; Beethoven-Haus 6, 7 top, 13, 20, 23, 24, 48, 51, 60, 62, 63 bottom, 66–67, 79 top, 85; Beethoven-Haus, H.C. Bodmer Collection 14, 22, 38 bottom; Bibliothèque Nationale 72–73; Bildarchiv Foto Marburg 88; Bildarchiv Preussischer Kulturbesitz 16 top, 21 bottom, 30, 91; Bridgeman Art Library 11, 38 top, 78, 79 bottom, 86–87; Collections of the prince of Liechtenstein, Vaduz Castle 18 top, 54, 55 bottom; EMI 90, 92–93; E.T. Archive 26, 27 top, 27 bottom, 31, 42–43, 50–51; Mary Evans Picture Library 21 top, 49 bottom, 57 bottom, 59, 83 bottom, 87 bottom, 89; Graphische Sammlung Albertina 12–13; Robert Harding Picture Library 18–19; Hulton-Deutsch Collection 58 bottom, 72 bottom; Hunterian Art Gallery, University of Glasgow 19; Larousse 53; Lauros-Giraudon 35 bottom; Mansell Collection 44 bottom, 47, 52, 58 top, 72 top; Museen der Stadt Wien 39; National Portrait Gallery 92; Österreichische Nationalbibliothek 8, 9 top, 9 bottom, 16 bottom, 17, 25 top, 29, 32, 32–33, 33, 36, 41 top, 41 bottom, 45, 55 top, 57 top, 61, 64–65, 65, 68, 76, 76–77, 80, 84; Polydor 74–75; Royal College of Music 56; Scala 15 bottom, 34, 71 bottom; Spectrum Colour Library 49 top, 63 top, 70; Staats- und Universitätsbibliothek, Hamburg 25 bottom; Stadtarchiv Bonn 10–11; Ullstein Bilderdienst 28–29, 36–37, 69 top, 69 bottom, 71 top; ZEFA 15 top